OUTBACK PANTRY

FOOD AND STORIES
FROM OUTBACK AUSTRALIA

hardie grant publishing

OUTBACK PANTRY

FOOD AND STORIES FROM OUTBACK AUSTRALIA

LYNTON TAPP

hardie grant publishing

CONTENTS

INTRODUCTION

I grew up in the Katherine region of outback Northern Territory, on a cattle station with my mum and dad and two sisters. I learned to ride a horse before I could walk and was working in the stock camp by the time I was ten, so it was only natural that I saw my future in continuing on at the family's cattle properties. I loved that life: living out in the middle of nowhere, producing your own food, cooking on a campfire, fishing, hunting. Absolutely everything about it was great.

As a young boy growing up in the outback I had an Aboriginal nanny. Her name was Barbara and she used to take me on walks through the bush and show me how to find bush food and teach me about native plants and animals. I remember eating bush bananas off the vines and looking for conkerberries. This was my introduction to native Australian produce.

Along with native food, I loved fishing, but mum and dad couldn't stand it. My uncles used to let me tag along with them on fishing trips down to the river and that's how I learned how to fish.

In my late teens and early twenties I was working in our local town as a carpenter while the mustering season was slow. I found myself enjoying takeaway food and soft drinks way too much, and before I knew it I had gained a few extra kilograms (quite a few). The only way I knew how to counter this was to start cooking healthy food for myself. Now, on a cattle station you eat a lot of meat and three veg—which is in itself quite healthy—but now that I'd decided to cook for myself I started to really teach myself the basics of nutrition.

When my younger sister saw the changes I had made through healthy cooking she asked if I would move to America to help care for her while she attended a spinal rehabilitation clinic after breaking her back. This is when food became the central part of my life: cooking for her three to four times a day, continually learning more about different cooking techniques and nutrition. I was hooked.

After the life-changing experience of being on *MasterChef Australia* I packed my bags and moved to Melbourne to pursue my love of food and cooking. Since then I have been working with Matt Germanchis—one of Australia's best chefs—who has helped me refine my skills and taught me things about cooking that I didn't even know were possible.

In this cookbook I have focused on the incredible farmers of the Northern Territory and what they do to ensure we get our amazing produce. I wouldn't have had such a great platform to make these recipes without all of them. Australian farmers are the unsung, and sometimes forgotten, people of our wonderful food ... and the most important.

BASIC EQUIPMENT & INGREDIENTS

Whatever kind of home cook you are, there is some basic equipment that will make cooking easier from the get go. In an ideal world we would all have every gadget, pot, pan and appliance that would fit into our endlessly spacious kitchens. Sadly, this isn't the case, so I have made a short list of essentials that will help you create beautiful food in your kitchen. I recommend spending the money initially to buy good quality kitchen equipment and you will not have to worry about it again.

CUTTING/CHOPPING/BLENDING

- chef's knife
- pairing knife/utility knife
- serrated knife
- chopping board
- food processor

A chef's knife—used for all types of slicing, chopping and cutting—is possibly the most important item in your kitchen. For ease, I would recommend high carbon stainless steel as you will not have to worry about stains or rust on the blade. The size of your hand and your arm will determine what size your blade should be: 15 cm, 20 cm or 25 cm (6 in, 8 in or 10 in) blades being the most common. For finer work, which requires greater control such as chopping herbs, slicing garlic or peeling vegetables, an 8–10 cm (3–4 in) pairing knife is best. Lastly, a serrated knife is good for slicing bread or overripe tomatoes. If you buy a good quality sharp knife it will last many years and hold its edge longer. Always keep your knives sharp—if you cannot sharpen your own knife take it to your local knife shop and get them to touch it up on their stones once every month or two. If you are on a budget and can only afford one knife make it a chef's knife—the best one you can afford.

A good chopping board is very important. Plastic boards are the best for cleaning and hygiene, however, they are a little tougher on your blades than a wooden chopping board. Whichever you choose, just ensure it is big enough to fit your chef's knife. A guide to gauging the right size chopping board is to lay your knife diagonally across the board: there should be a 5–8 cm (2–3 in) space at each end of the knife.

I use a food processor a lot in my recipes as it cuts down prep time and helps produce a better final product. If you can't afford a food processor, an immersion blender will do.

COOKWARE/BAKEWARE

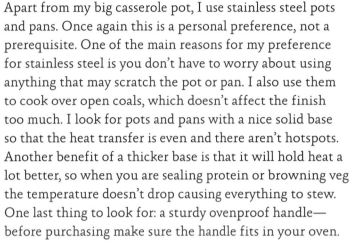

- 18 cm (7 in) saucepan
- 24 cm (9½ in) stew pot
- 26 cm (10¼ in) frying pan
- 35 cm (14 in) roasting tray
- 43 cm (17 in) baking tray
- 7.5 litre (253 fl oz) stockpot
- large cast iron casserole pot

Apart from my big casserole pot, I use stainless steel pots and pans. Once again this is a personal preference, not a prerequisite. One of the main reasons for my preference for stainless steel is you don't have to worry about using anything that may scratch the pot or pan. I also use them to cook over open coals, which doesn't affect the finish too much. I look for pots and pans with a nice solid base so that the heat transfer is even and there aren't hotspots. Another benefit of a thicker base is that it will hold heat a lot better, so when you are sealing protein or browning veg the temperature doesn't drop causing everything to stew. One last thing to look for: a sturdy ovenproof handle—before purchasing make sure the handle fits in your oven.

TOOLS

- 500 ml–1 litre (17 fl oz–34 fl oz) measuring jug
- box grater
- electric scales
- fine sieve or tamis
- mandoline
- measuring cup set
- measuring spoon set
- set of stainless steel mixing bowls
- spatula
- tongs
- vegetable peeler
- wooden spoon

The tools list could be a long one, so I have only listed my most-used equipment. Everyone has a different list, so just use this as a guide, not a rule. Your own list will definitely grow as you continue to cook more and more. This will be a useful start, though.

THE PANTRY

A well stocked pantry goes a long way to making cooking and entertaining easier. If, tucked away in your pantry, you already have the perfect sauce to go with your meal, or a great jam ready for when you want scones, or some pickled veg next time you want to add something different to a dish, you are already halfway to a great meal. I have included here some of my favourite recipes that help me around the kitchen, however I would encourage you to grow your own repertoire and design a pantry list that suits you. I have a few tips when cooking that I thought I might share, they are not earth-shattering discoveries, but I think they are helpful nonetheless.

First things first: start with good quality oils. Don't feel that you have to use extra virgin olive oil for everything, just as long as you are not buying some import that has either undercut our local producers or been produced at the cost of the environment, or both. I use good vegetable oil a lot in high-heat cooking as it doesn't burn and won't impart an overpowering taste—save the extra virgin for finishing a dish.

Good quality salt is important, I believe, only when finishing the dish. It is also expensive. I use standard cooking salt at the start of the cooking process, such as when seasoning meat or making a cure mix, but when it comes to serving the dish I use a good quality sea salt.

I recommend making a good quality stock at home—stock is the basis of so many amazing dishes so it is worth the effort. It is simple, cheap and will last for months in your freezer. By making a big batch of stock at home you are not only saving money but you will also know that you are not putting any preservatives into your food.

Use good quality dairy. Make sure it is coming from your local dairy farmers, or at the very least try not to buy the cheap milk. By buying good quality dairy you will not only be putting much needed money back into the dairy industry but also ensuring that you are buying a superior product.

Eggs. I don't need to talk about eggs, you all know what to do. Organic and free range. Don't fall for marketing ploys and get cage-free: some of those places can be as bad as caged egg factories. Look for eggs that come from a real farm where the chickens are free to roam—if you know the farmer and can buy from them directly, perfect.

DAMPER

Every camp cook has his or her secret variation of the classic damper, which makes it unique. But I would have to say that while growing up, our camp cook had the best recipe—or as he would humbly say, 'It's probably not the best, but in the top three!' As a kid I was banned from going near the damper at smoko time because of a string of unfortunate events, mostly me hacking into a freshly baked damper and ruining it for the whole camp … to this day I am wary of cutting bread unsupervised. Served warm with butter and golden syrup, damper transports me back to my childhood, sitting with a bunch of rugged country men enjoying a break from drafting cattle in the yards with a cup of billy tea. Bear in mind that throughout the whole mixing process you need to work the dough as quickly as possible, this will make for a lighter end product. It also helps to work in a cool kitchen.

90 g (3 oz) unsalted butter, extra chilled

40 g (⅓ cup) powdered milk

450 g (1 lb/3 cups) self-raising flour

1 teaspoon table salt

380 ml (12 fl oz/1 ⅓ cup) cold beer

Preheat oven to 200 °C (400 °F).

In a large mixing bowl knead the butter into the flour, powdered milk and salt until the mixture resembles breadcrumbs. Pour the beer over the mixture and work the dough until it has just come together. Turn the dough onto a floured surface and knead it briefly until the dough becomes smooth. Shape into a 16 cm dome and transfer to a lined baking tray. Cut 1 cm deep slices into the top in your desired pattern—the cuts will stop the crust from cracking during the baking period.

Bake for 25–30 minutes, or until there is a hollow sound when the base is tapped. Once cooked, allow to cool for 5 minutes. Damper is best served warm and fresh with a selection of your favourite toppings. My recommendation would be with butter and golden syrup.

For a sweet variation of this recipe use milk as your wet ingredient, add 3 tablespoons of sugar and half a cup of your favourite dry fruit.

BUTTER

MAKES APPROXIMATELY 180 G

It is such a simple task to make your own butter and it will be better than any you can buy in the supermarket. Making your own butter is a must when you have made a beautiful loaf of bread or have just taken a batch of perfect scones from the oven.

500 ml (17 fl oz/2 cups) good
quality organic thickened
(whipping) cream
500 ml (17 fl oz/2 cups) chilled
water

Whip the cream in a large mixing bowl with an electric mixer on low. As the cream begins to form medium peaks put your mixer on high and continue to beat the cream until it begins to split, this will take about 10 minutes. Once the cream has split, turn the mixer off. Drain, and discard the whey. Fill the bowl with half of the chilled water and mix on low for a further 30 seconds, drain water and repeat. Remove the butter from the bowl and squeeze in your hands, like squeezing the water out of a wet rag, to remove excess liquid.

The butter is now ready. You can use this straight away or store it in an airtight container in the fridge for up to a week.

WATTLE SEED BUTTER

MAKES 140 G

I make this compound butter to spread on warm pancakes, damper muffins, scones … pretty much for any sweet baking I do, I have some of this butter on hand to generously smear about.

100 g (3½ oz) unsalted butter
1½ tablespoons ground wattle
seed
¼ teaspoon ground coffee
2 tablespoons maple syrup

In a food processor or mixer with a paddle attachment, beat the butter with the maple syrup until pale and creamy. Turn the motor off and add the coffee and wattle seed, then stir in with a spatula until rippled through. If you overmix this butter it will turn brown from the coffee—it will still taste fine, just look unattractive. Roll it into a log with baking paper and store in the fridge for up to a week, or in the freezer for a month.

CHICKEN STOCK

MAKES 4 LITRES

1.5 kg (3 lb 5 oz) chicken
   carcasses (get these from your
   local butcher)
1 onion, thinly sliced
1 carrot, thinly sliced
4 stalks celery
2 bay leaves
5 white peppercorns
4 litres (135 fl oz/16 cups) cold
   water

Place all ingredients in a large stockpot and cover with the water. Bring the stock to boil, then reduce to simmer. Continue to simmer stock for 2 hours, skimming regularly to remove any fat and debris that rises to the surface.

Once the stock has finished cooking, pour it through a fine sieve, reserving the liquid and discarding the solids. Cool immediately. Chicken stock can last in the fridge for up to four days or in the freezer for up to four months.

VEAL STOCK

MAKES 4 LITRES

1.5 kg (3 lb 5 oz) veal bones
1 onion, thinly sliced
2 carrots, thinly sliced
2 stalks celery, thinly sliced
4 litres (135 fl oz/16 cups) cold
   water
5 black peppercorns
2 bay leaves

Preheat the oven to 200 °C (400 °F).

Place the veal bones and vegetables in separate heavy roasting trays. Cook in the oven for 1½ hours, turning every 30 minutes.

Once the bones and vegetables are browned, transfer to a large pot or stockpot that will hold all the ingredients. Pour the water in and add the peppercorns and bay leaves.

On a stovetop bring stock to boil. Reduce heat to simmer and cook for 2 hours, skimming periodically to remove any fat so that you have a clear stock.

Once the stock is finished cooking, strain it through a fine sieve. Discard the solids and reserve the liquid, and cool immediately. Fresh stock can last in the fridge for up to four days or in the freezer for up to four months.

CURING SALT

MAKES 500 G

I use curing salt when I am preparing raw seafood dishes. Curing times vary: for a whole salmon or ocean trout I will completely cover it with curing salt for 22–24 hours, but for a snapper or pearl meat tartar I will cure the meat for only 25–30 minutes. Add different herbs, spices and seasoning to infuse any flavour you like.

300 g (10½ oz/2¼ cups) good
    quality grey sea salt
200 g (7 oz/1 cup) caster
    (superfine) sugar
grated zest of 2 lemons
grated zest of ½ an orange

In a mixing bowl combine all the ingredients thoroughly. Use a spatula or your hands to really work the mix so that the zests are evenly dispersed. Store in an airtight container in your fridge for up to three months.

CURRY PASTE

SERVES 2

Curry paste is an essential for me. What you don't use, you can just freeze for later. You can also use this paste to coat your favourite fish and bake it in a medium oven.

1 teaspoon coriander seeds
1 teaspoon freshly ground black
    pepper
1 teaspoon cumin seeds
1 stick lemongrass
3 banana shallots, peeled
4 garlic cloves, peeled
3 cm (1¼ in) galangal, peeled
½ cup fresh coriander, roots and
    stems
2 teaspoons belacan (shrimp paste)
2 tablespoons dried shrimp
long red chillies, to taste
2 kaffir lime leaves
125 ml (4 fl oz/½ cup) peanut oil

In a dry, hot frying pan toast the coriander seeds, black pepper and cumin seeds until fragrant. Transfer to a mortar and pestle, and grind to a fine powder. Thinly slice the lemongrass and add to the spice mix in the mortar. Grind to a fine paste.

Transfer the lemongrass paste to a large food processor and add the remaining ingredients. Process until a smooth paste has formed.

Heat a non-stick frying pan on low–medium and add the curry paste. Gently cook, without burning, for 20–25 minutes. Cooking the curry paste slowly is important to ensure there is no raw onion or garlic flavour, and to enhance the natural sweetness of the ingredients. Store in an airtight container in your fridge for a week, or in your freezer for up to three months.

LOUISIANA-STYLE HOT SAUCE (UNFERMENTED)

MAKES 750 ML

This is a very simple hot sauce. If you are a chilli enthusiast and love the taste and heat of chillies then this is a sauce you should make. When you make this recipe, Craig from Darwin Chilli Co. (see pages 12–13) suggests you use the type of chilli that you like to eat because it will taste exactly like the chilli you use.

500 g (1 lb 2 oz) whole hot red
  chillies, stems removed
250 ml (8½ fl oz/1 cup) white
  vinegar
1 tablespoon table salt

In a large blender or food processor blend all the ingredients for 4–5 minutes, until everything is finely chopped.

Transfer to a large pot and bring the ingredients to boil over high heat. Reduce the heat to a gentle simmer and cook for a further 12–14 minutes.

Pass the hot sauce through a fine sieve, and bottle in sterilised containers. It will last up to three months in the fridge.

CRAIG'S BARBECUE SAUCE

MAKES APPROXIMATELY 2.5 LITRES

Craig's advice on this simple barbecue sauce recipe is to use good quality brewed coffee that you drink, whether that be espresso, percolated or instant.

500 g (1 lb 2 oz) tomato paste, or
  good quality tomato 'ketchup'
500 g (1 lb 2 oz/2¼ cups) soft
  brown sugar
500 ml (17 fl oz/2 cups) white
  vinegar
1 litre (34 fl oz/4 cups) black coffee
2 tablespoons ground black pepper
2 tablespoons table salt

Transfer all the ingredients into a large pot and blend with a stick blender for 3–4 minutes, until everything is thoroughly combined.

Bring the ingredients to boil over high heat. Once boiling reduce to a simmer and cook for 15–20 minutes.

Cool the sauce and then bottle in sterilised containers. The sauce will last up to two months in the fridge.

DARWIN CHILLI CO.
Craig Zwetsloot

Craig Zwetsloot created a humble business in 2010 called Darwin Chilli Co. It was a combination of his love of hot food, hotter chillies and a string of events that saw him have one of the biggest crops in Australia of the world's hottest chilli.

Craig is a proud descendant of the Ceylonese Burghers, and chillies and cooking have always been part of his life. Living in Darwin for the past twenty years, Craig found himself in the unusual position of not being able to find a chilli hot enough for his tastes. To the annoyance of all the local Thai ladies, he would buy every fresh fruit and veg market out of chillies every weekend to make sauce for

himself, and his friends and family. The idea of turning his chilli sauce into a business came to him when he was gifted a secret crop of habanero chillies by a woman whose only request was that he make her some 'sweet chilli sauce' in return. Obviously, it went against every bone in Craig's body to make a 'sweet' chilli sauce, so he made a sauce of his own creation, which everyone loved, and turned the idea into a business.

In 2011 Craig was among a group of importers bringing rare chillies into Australia to meet the demand for extra hot chillies. One of the chilli crops Craig grew was a Trinidad Scorpion. When it was announced as the world's hottest chilli later that year, chillies were out of season in the southern states of Australia and Craig found himself with the largest crop

in the country. Business exploded: he was selling chilli seeds to over fourteen different countries around the world for $1 a seed.

Initially Craig was selling his sauces online internationally and Australia-wide, however being a proud local he decided to take the term 'support local' to a new level and now only sells his sauces within the Northern Territory, personally, or via a select few distributors. He says he just didn't like the impersonal nature of packing sauce bottles into a carton and sending them off. Craig appreciates a genuine conversation and handshake, especially since all of his sauces are handmade and individually bottled by hand.

PRESERVED CHILLIES

For best results when preserving chillies, or any fruit or vegetable, you should use home grown or organic chemical-free produce. This will ensure the preserving process will not be inhibited by other chemicals or preserving agents.

500 g (1 lb 2 oz) long red chillies
190 g (6½ oz/¾ cup) table salt
1 teaspoon black peppercorns
1 lemon, quartered
3 bay leaves
juice of 4 lemons
1 tablespoon olive oil
You will also need a 1 litre
    (34 fl oz/4 cup) sterilised glass
    jar with a non-corrosive lid
    (plastic is best)

Start by removing the tops and ends of the chillies, this will make the preserving process quicker. When all the chillies have had their ends trimmed place them into the glass jar with salt, peppercorns, lemon quarters and bay leaves.

Pour the lemon juice over the chillies and fill the rest of the jar with water, leaving enough space to add the olive oil. The olive oil will act as a barrier and stop any mould developing. Date the jar and store in a cool dark place. The preserved chillies will be ready in three to four weeks, but the flavour will improve with time.

PICKLING LIQUID

400 ml (13½ fl oz/1⅔ cups) good
  quality white wine vinegar
150 ml (5 fl oz/⅔ cup) water
200 g (7 oz/1 cup) caster
  (superfine) sugar
1 teaspoon whole coriander seeds
3 tablespoons dill

Heat the vinegar, water, sugar and coriander seeds in a saucepan over high heat until the sugar has dissolved. Remove the pickling liquid from the heat and add the dill. Let cool and store in an airtight container. If stored in a clean airtight container the pickling liquid can last up to three months in the fridge.

PICKLED SPRING ONIONS

To make pickled spring onions (scallion), use the white part only, cut on a bias and trim any roots. Completely submerge in pickling liquid in a saucepan over medium heat. Gently simmer for 8–10 minutes, or until the spring onions just start to soften. Cool and store in a sterilised jar in the fridge for up to three months.

PICKLED CABBAGE

Thinly slice green cabbage and generously season with salt. Place in a colander for 20 minutes to let the excess water that is released from the cabbage drain off. Rinse thoroughly with water, pat dry and place in a sterilised jar. Cover with pickling liquid and seal. Store in the fridge for up to three months.

PICKLED CUCUMBERS

Thinly slice cucumbers lengthways using a mandoline, submerge into pickling liquid and let sit for an hour before using.

SALAD DRESSING

A very simple and versatile salad dressing, suitable
for something as delicate as dressed leaves or your
favourite beetroot and goat's cheese salad.

80 ml (2½ fl oz/⅓ cup) extra virgin
   olive oil
1 teaspoon seeded mustard
1 teaspoon honey
1 tablespoon lemon juice
3 teaspoons chardonnay vinegar
1 teaspoon white wine vinegar
pinch of sea salt

In a small mixing bowl combine all the ingredients
thoroughly with a whisk. This salad dressing will last
up to one week in the fridge in an airtight container.
If you want it to last longer substitute a good quality
light vinegar for the lemon juice, it will last up to two
weeks in the fridge if you do this.

AIOLI

3 egg yolks
1 tablespoon apple cider vinegar
1 tablespoon lemon juice
2 teaspoons dijon mustard
½ garlic clove, finely grated
1½ teaspoons table salt
300 ml (10 fl oz/1¼ cups)
    vegetable oil
100 ml (3½ fl oz/⅓ cup) extra
    virgin olive oil

In a food processor combine all the ingredients excluding the oils. Process for 10 seconds. With the motor running very slowly, add the oils until completely emulsified.

Transfer the aioli to an airtight container, placing plastic wrap on the surface so that a skin does not form. Refrigerate immediately. The aioli is ready to use once cool. Do not keep fresh aioli for more than three days.

LEMON VINAIGRETTE

I use this versatile dressing all the time: I season cooked fish with it, drizzle it over vegetables from the garden and, of course, use it as a light dressing in salads.

2½ tablespoons extra virgin olive oil
1½ tablespoons fresh lemon juice
1 teaspoon dijon mustard
pinch of sea salt

In a small mixing bowl combine the ingredients thoroughly with a whisk. This dressing will last two to three days in an airtight container in the fridge.

DATE CHUTNEY

MAKES 550–600 G

I always have a jar of this chutney in the fridge. Its flavour
goes well with almost any cold meat sandwich. I even use it
as a sauce alternative for pies and sausage rolls. The natural
sugars from the dates mean that you don't need a truckload
of caster (superfine) sugar like most chutneys to make this.
I wouldn't say it's clean eating, but it's a start.

1 brown onion, finely sliced

1 tablespoon grape seed oil, or
    any neutral-tasting oil

2 tomatoes, roughly diced

1 teaspoon ground cumin

1 teaspoon sweet paprika

½ teaspoon smoked paprika

½ teaspoon freshly ground black
    pepper

½ teaspoon ground cinnamon

1½ teaspoons table salt

80 ml (2½ fl oz/⅓ cup) apple cider
    vinegar

250 ml (8½ fl oz/1 cup) water

250 g (9 oz) pitted dates

In a saucepan over a medium–high heat, sweat the onions
with the grape seed oil until they are intensely caramelised,
this should take between 10–15 minutes. Once the onions
are browned, add the chopped tomato and cook for a
further 10 minutes, stirring occasionally.

Add the spice mix and cook until the onion and tomato
mix starts to stick to the bottom of the pan. Before the
spices start to burn, add the vinegar, water and dates.
Be sure to dislodge any spices stuck to the bottom of the
saucepan with a wooden spoon.

Cook the date chutney gently for a further 20–25 minutes,
or until most of the liquid has evaporated. Transfer the
chutney to a large food processor and process to a
consistency of your liking. I like a chunky mix and only
give my chutney 35–40 seconds in my food processor.

Transfer the date chutney to sterilised jars, and date and
label. Once cool, store in the fridge for up to six weeks.

SHORTCRUST PASTRY

450 G

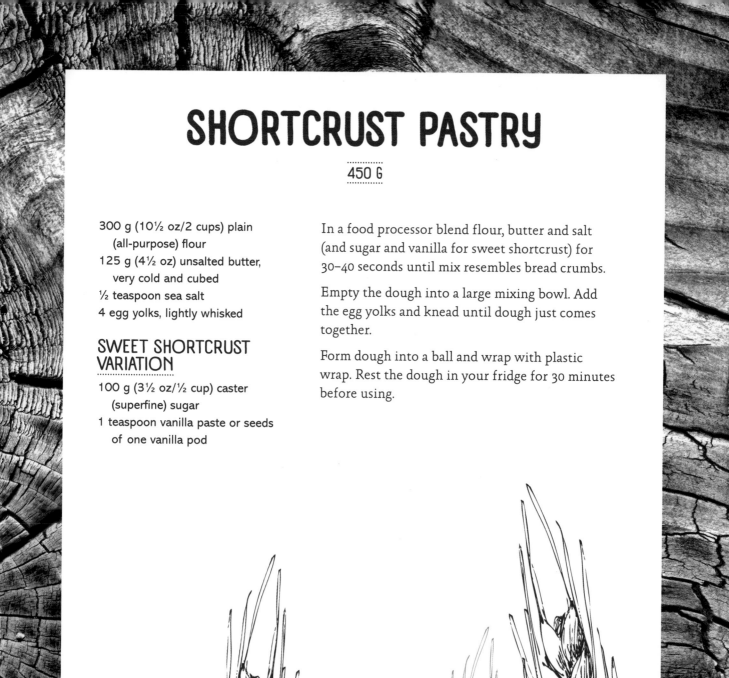

300 g (10½ oz/2 cups) plain
   (all-purpose) flour
125 g (4½ oz) unsalted butter,
   very cold and cubed
½ teaspoon sea salt
4 egg yolks, lightly whisked

SWEET SHORTCRUST VARIATION

100 g (3½ oz/½ cup) caster
   (superfine) sugar
1 teaspoon vanilla paste or seeds
   of one vanilla pod

In a food processor blend flour, butter and salt
(and sugar and vanilla for sweet shortcrust) for
30–40 seconds until mix resembles bread crumbs.

Empty the dough into a large mixing bowl. Add
the egg yolks and knead until dough just comes
together.

Form dough into a ball and wrap with plastic
wrap. Rest the dough in your fridge for 30 minutes
before using.

APRICOT JAM

500 g (1 lb 2 oz/2¾ cups) dried
  apricots
55 g (2 oz/¼ cup) caster
  (superfine) sugar
1½ cups (12½ fl oz) orange juice,
  good quality organic

Place the ingredients into a saucepan—if you have a jam pan use it—and bring the apricots to boil. Cook for 30–35 minutes, until two-thirds of the liquid has evaporated and the apricots are falling apart.

Transfer the mixture to a food processor and puree the jam to the consistency you like. I like mine quite rough and rustic. If the jam seems runny continue to cook off the liquid until you have reached your desired consistency, remembering that the jam will set further once cooled.

Transfer jam to sterilised jars and seal. The apricot jam will last up to a month in the fridge.

BROWN SAUCE

MAKES 250 ML

I use this brown sauce with almost any type of meat and poultry. If you are roasting anything, simply strain off the pan juices and add it to your brown sauce for added flavour.

2 tablespoons vegetable oil
1 kg (2 lb 3 oz) brown onions,
  thinly sliced
200 g (7 oz) beef scraps
3 star anise
1 stick cinnamon
375 ml (12½ fl oz/1½ cups) red
  wine (the wine you drink)
500 ml (17 fl oz/2 cups) chicken
  stock
500 ml (17 fl oz/2 cups) veal stock

In a large saucepan over a medium–hot stove, heat the oil and brown the onions and beef scraps with the star anise and cinnamon stick. It is important to cook the onions and beef until they are dark brown, but not burnt, as this creates a rich flavour in the final sauce.

Once the onions and beef scraps are caramelised pour in the red wine and reduce by two-thirds. Add all the chicken and veal stock and bring to boil. Once the brown sauce is boiling, lower the heat to a gentle simmer and reduce the sauce until there is about a cup of liquid remaining. Strain the brown sauce through a fine sieve, reserving the liquid and discarding the solids.

VEGETABLES AND LEAVES

VEGETABLES AND LEAVES

Growing up in an environment where you would only go to the supermarkets once a month drastically influenced what we would be able to buy as fresh ingredients. Tinned vegetables were a large part of my diet, as the only vegetables that we would consider buying fresh were potatoes, onions and pumpkin (winter squash). If you wanted anything outside of these staples it was tinned.

Every now and then my mother would start a vegetable patch and try to grow some fresh vegetables for the station. It was always so much fun growing our own vegetables, not to mention a learning experience. However, it is fair to say that our family weren't the best gardeners—some may use the term stone-thumbs to describe us—and eventually the good ol' vegie patch would succumb to weeds and lack of attention. Thankfully the farming community in the Northern Territory is far more talented at growing crops than we were at vegie patches.

Whether in the Top End or the Red Centre, I always find it astonishing what grows throughout the Northern Territory. The tropical Top End is undoubtedly known for its Asian veg, which are cultivated and sold at local markets and throughout Australia. Going to a local market in Darwin is an incredible experience, any ingredient you could want to use in South-East Asian cooking is there, all of which is grown within an hour of Darwin. Whether it be snake (yard long) beans, eggplants (aubergine), sweet potatoes, ginger, curry leaves or okra, it grows easily and in abundance.

But the Territory is not limited to Asian veg. As you start heading south, away from Darwin, into the dryer, cooler climate, there are a range of different crops that are grown. Pumpkins (winter squash) are famous around the Katherine region: crops as far as the eye can see.

The Red Centre is undoubtedly best known for native Australian ingredients and rightly so with bush oranges, wild potatoes and onion, bush bananas, native bush tomatoes and dessert limes to name just a few. A number of these native Australian ingredients are foraged by local Aboriginal people and sold commercially. A company based in Alice Springs even grows brassicas and lettuces. Now this may not seem very impressive, but when you consider the weather of Alice Springs and the fact that it is considered to be in a desert, with a low rainfall and the varying temperatures that come with being a desert, you can see why I am fascinated by the beautiful Red Centre.

SHAVED BROCCOLI AND BURRATA SALAD

SERVES 4

Burrata is found in specialty grocers and delis, and is a form of
mozzarella cheese with a mix of cream and mozzarella in the centre.
If you cannot find burrata cheese you can use plain mozzarella.

2 broccoli
2 tablespoons lemon vinaigrette
   (see page 20)
2 teaspoons extra lemon juice
pinch of table salt
2 pieces (200 g) burrata cheese
2 tablespoons toasted hazelnuts,
   roughly chopped
freshly ground white pepper, to
   serve

Bring a pot of salted water to boil on the stovetop.

Cut small broccoli florets from the stem and set the stems
aside. In the boiling water blanch the florets for 2 minutes,
or until just softened. Strain the florets through a sieve
immediately, discarding the water, and run under cool
water to prevent overcooking. Place in a large mixing bowl.

Shave the broccoli stems into thin ribbons with a vegetable
peeler or mandoline, and place in the mixing bowl with the
blanched florets. Pour the vinaigrette and extra lemon
juice over the broccoli and add the pinch of salt. Toss the
broccoli well, until evenly dressed.

To serve the salad, place the broccoli onto a serving plate
and tear the fresh burrata cheese over the top. Sprinkle
with the chopped hazelnuts and, lastly, season with white
pepper before eating.

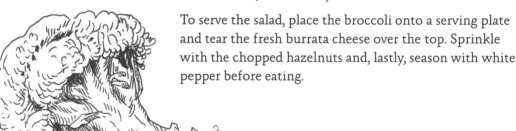

THE UNLOVED ICEBERG SALAD

SERVES 4

Everyone has gone off iceberg lettuce over the years,
but I think it's a great lettuce and I use it all the time.
It's cheap and refreshing. It lends itself to a lot of dishes,
whether it be in a burger, a salad bowl or even grilled.
Serve everything in this salad cold on a hot summer's day.

DRESSING

2 teaspoons buttermilk
2 teaspoons sour cream
½ teaspoon dijon mustard
½ teaspoon honey
1 teaspoon chardonnay vinegar
¼ teaspoon sea salt
⅛ teaspoon freshly ground black
    pepper
3 teaspoons chives, chopped

½ head of iceberg lettuce, cut
    into wedges
50 g (1¾ oz) of your favourite
    blue cheese, crumbled

In a small bowl whisk together the ingredients for the dressing until well combined. Lay the iceberg wedges on a serving platter or board, and drizzle with the dressing. Lastly, crumble the blue cheese over the top.

ZUCCHINI SALAD

This is a very simple raw salad that takes minutes to prepare.
However be sure to make this salad just before serving, as once
the lemon juice and salt is added the zucchini (courgette) will
begin to break down and lose a lot of its beautiful flavour.

4 large zucchinis (courgettes)
2 teaspoons chilli flakes
½ teaspoon sea salt
½ teaspoon freshly ground black
   pepper
2½ tablespoons lemon juice
½ cup mint leaves, loosely packed
2 long red chillies, seeds removed
   and thinly sliced

Grate the zucchinis (courgettes) into a large ceramic
mixing bowl using the largest grating side on your box
grater. Add the chilli flakes, salt, pepper and lemon juice,
and toss well to combine. Serve immediately, tearing the
mint leaves and scattering them and the fresh chilli over
the top. If you are inclined, you can drizzle extra virgin
olive oil over the top at this stage.

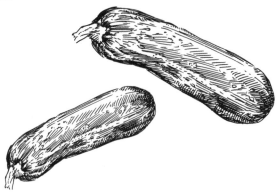

KOHLRABI AND NASHI SALAD WITH LIME DRESSING

SERVES 4 AS A SIDE SALAD

This dish is a great simple and quick summertime salad. The kohlrabi and lime really freshen up a hot day, and the sweet juicy nashi pear is a great accompaniment.

1 bulb kohlrabi
2 nashi pears
2 limes
1 tablespoon fish sauce
1 teaspoon freshly ground white pepper
½ cup Thai basil leaves

I prepare the kohlrabi using a vegetable peeler, however a box grater works just as well. Peel the skin from the kohlrabi and discard. Continue to peel the kohlrabi, placing the shavings into a mixing bowl.

On the largest grating side of your grater, grate the nashi pear lengthways until you reach the core. Discard the core. Prepare the nashi pear as quickly as you can, as it will begin to oxidize and discolour immediately. This will not affect the taste, just the presentation of the final salad.

In a large salad bowl combine the kohlrabi shavings and grated nashi. Squeeze the juice of both limes over the salad and add the fish sauce. Add the white pepper, mix well and serve with the Thai basil torn and sprinkled over the top.

GRILLED BABY COS WITH ANCHOVIES AND LEMON

SERVES 4

I see salads all the time with anchovies and aged cheese and lots of vinegar, and I always think that the leaf that is being used is lost in the background. This recipe is influenced in part from my childhood and in part from my love of American barbecue. Enjoy with a summer beer.

2 baby cos (romaine) lettuce
3 tablespoons extra virgin olive oil
pinch of table salt
8 anchovy fillets, cut in half
    lengthways
2 teaspoons capers, washed
1½ tablespoons lemon juice
3 hard-boiled eggs, whites
    removed and discarded, yolks
    roughly chopped
25 g (1 oz/¼ cup) shaved
    parmesan, to serve

Preheat a chargrill pan over high heat.

Remove any tough or broken outer leaves from the baby cos (romaine), then cut each one in half lengthways. Evenly season all of the cos with 1 tablespoon of the olive oil and the salt. Place the cos, cut-side down, onto the hot chargrill pan and, without turning, cook each cos until it has grill marks and starts to blacken. Remove the cos halves from the pan and set aside to cool slightly.

While the cos is cooling it's time to make the dressing. Roughly chop the capers and place into a small mixing bowl. Pour in the remaining 2 tablespoons of olive oil and the lemon juice, and mix gently with a fork to combine.

To serve, place the cos halves on a serving tray, and drizzle with the caper dressing. Finally, top with anchovies, shaved parmesan cheese and chopped boiled egg yolks.

PUMPKIN FARMER

John Shaw

At an unassuming farm not far from Katherine resides John Shaw, a local pumpkin farmer. John hails from a long line of horticultural farmers who have a proud family history extending back over a hundred years. Working on the family citrus and stone fruit farm in South Australia since he was six years old, John decided to use his extensive knowledge and history in farming to start a new life in the Northern Territory and in 1995, at the young age of twenty-four, he made the move.

He took the essentials: clothes, a car and three tractors, and bought 180 hectares (444 acres) with his life's savings just outside of Katherine. Initially he put his hand to growing everything to make an income so he could reinvest back into his property. When I say everything, he literally grew all you could in the Northern Territory: capsicums (bell peppers), onions, zucchinis (courgettes), chillies, eggplants (aubergines), tomatoes, pumpkins (winter squash), melons and cucumbers.

Over the years John has moved his business towards mainly producing pumpkins, onions and melons. In a bumper season John will produce 500 tonnes of pumpkins, along with Spanish onions and melons. For John, growing pumpkins in the Northern Territory means that he supplies Australia when the southern crops aren't producing any pumpkins. Pumpkins travel well and handle the heat after picking a lot better than other crops.

Every pumpkin on his property is picked by hand, all 500 tonnes of them. This is done by only six staff during the picking season to ensure that the best quality product is delivered to John's customers.

John is passionate about farming and ensuring a bright future for the agricultural industry and finds himself in his (very little) spare time as the chairman of the Nuffield Farming Scholarship, which sends young farmers from around Australia overseas to experience and learn farming techniques from farming industries around the world. The young scholarship winners then return to Australia sharing what they have learned and enhancing the industry.

GREEN PAPAYA AND PRAWN SALAD

SERVES 3–4

This is one of my all-time favourites. Nothing reminds me more of
the markets around Darwin than a freshly made green papaya salad.
I like to add pork scratchings and prawns to mine — after all, I am
a meat lover — however, it is just as good without if you prefer.

2 teaspoons peanut oil

50 g (1¾ oz) Chinese sausage
(lap cheong), thinly sliced

6 large raw tiger prawns (shrimp),
peeled and deveined

200 g (7 oz) green papaya, peeled
and finely grated

1 large carrot, peeled and finely
grated

100 g (3½ oz) daikon, peeled and
finely grated

70 g (2½ oz) pork scratchings
(crackling), you can make your
own or buy it from Asian
supermarkets

pinch of table salt

2 tablespoons coriander (cilantro)
leaves, torn

2 tablespoons Vietnamese mint,
torn

DRESSING

60 ml (2 fl oz/¼ cup) lime juice

1 tablespoon fish sauce

1 tablespoon palm sugar (jaggery),
finely chopped

1 red Thai chilli

½ garlic clove, finely grated

1 tablespoon coriander root

I prefer to prepare this salad using a mandoline with a fine
grater attachment, but a box grater or julienne peeler will
work just as well.

Preheat a sauté pan over medium–high heat. Add the
peanut oil to the pan and allow to heat up. Add the
Chinese sausage and sauté for 1–2 minutes allowing some
of the fat in the sausage to render out. Once the sausage
has started to release its fat add the prawns (shrimp) and
cook for a further 3–4 minutes, or until cooked through,
turning regularly. Remove the Chinese sausage and prawns
and place on paper towel to absorb some of the fat. When
the prawns have cooled slightly cut in half lengthways.

Place all the dressing ingredients into a food processor and
blend for 1–2 minutes. Adjust the seasoning of the dressing
at this point—the time of year and brand of ingredients
will determine the balance of the dressing. A tip is to have
backup lime juice, fish sauce and palm sugar (jaggery) to
readjust the seasoning.

In a mixing bowl combine the raw salad ingredients and
pour the dressing over the top. Place this onto a serving
platter and pile the Chinese sausage and prawns on top,
then the crushed pork scratchings and, lastly, sprinkle with
the torn coriander (cilantro) and Vietnamese mint.

PUMPKIN DUMPLINGS

SERVES 6 AS A SIDE DISH

This variation of potato gnocchi works great with pork and most tomato-based ragu, just be mindful that with the lower starch content they can be quite delicate. Be gentle with this mix, I won't judge you if you use a little extra flour to stiffen the dough the first couple of times you try this recipe—but do remember, you are making pumpkin (winter squash) dumplings not flour ones.

550 g (1 lb 3 oz) butternut pumpkin (winter squash)

150 g (5½ oz) royal blue potatoes, or any other mashing variety

3 egg yolks

½ teaspoon table salt

½ teaspoon nutmeg, freshly grated

½ teaspoon ground white pepper

¼ cup manchego cheese, finely grated

110 g (4 oz/¾ cup) plain (all-purpose) flour, plus extra flour for dusting

Preheat oven to 160 °C (320 °F).

Peel and cut the pumpkin (winter squash) into 4cm (1½ in) pieces. Place the pumpkin flesh-side down, along with the whole unpeeled royal blue potatoes on a lined baking tray and bake for 50–60 minutes, or until the potatoes and pumpkin are completely soft when pierced with a fork. Remove from the oven and cool uncovered.

When the pumpkin and potato are cool enough to handle, mash the pumpkin in a large mixing bowl and peel the potato and pass it through a potato ricer or fine sieve into the mixing bowl with the pumpkin. Add the egg yolks, salt, nutmeg, white pepper and manchego, and gently combine with a pastry card or spatula. Slowly start to incorporate the flour until a semi-firm dough is formed. Too much flour will make gluey dumplings so try to use just enough flour so that you can form the dough.

Dust a clean, lined baking tray with flour ready for the prepped gnocchi.

Turn the pumpkin mixture onto a floured bench and divide evenly into four portions. Roll each portion into 2 cm thick logs. Dust the pumpkin logs with flour so that they are easier to handle once cut. Cut the logs into 2 cm pieces and transfer to the floured baking tray.

Bring a large pot of heavily salted water to boil on the stove. Cook the gnocchi in batches for 2–3 minutes each. As each batch is ready transfer it to a warm, buttered saucepan until all the gnocchi is cooked. Serve immediately.

CHILLI FRIED MARKET GREENS

SERVES 6

This recipe is more about the technique than the ingredients.
It's a dish that I make if I'm starting to feel under the weather
or have veg that needs to be used up. It's great for breakfast
with a poached egg or as the 'greens' for any dinner.

2 tablespoons vegetable oil
200 g (7 oz) green beans, trimmed
200 g (7 oz) broccolini, trimmed
2 garlic cloves, peeled and bruised
100 g (3½ oz) cavolo nero, stalks
    removed
1½ teaspoons chilli flakes
1 teaspoon sea salt
juice of ½ a lemon
50 g (1¾ oz/½ cup) flaked
    almonds, toasted

Heat the vegetable oil in a sauté pan over high heat.
When the oil is hot add the green beans, broccolini and
garlic. Cook for 2 minutes, constantly moving the pan.
Add the cavolo nero, chilli and salt. Continue to sauté
for a further 2 minutes, or until the broccolini is tender
and cavolo nero is wilted.

Add the lemon juice. Serve immediately, scattering the
almonds over the top.

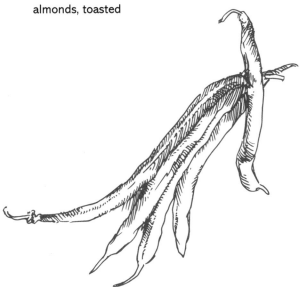

CHARRED CAULIFLOWER AND TAHINI SALAD

SERVES 4

Cauliflower is a vegetable that should be used a lot more. It is so versatile and can be used in pretty much any cuisine. It stands by itself as a lovely ingredient or can be put with a whole bunch of different flavours as I have in this recipe. Don't think of it as something just for dieters or cheese bakes.

100 g (3½ oz) tinned chickpeas
2 teaspoons table salt
3 tablespoons olive oil
2 teaspoons cumin powder
1 large cauliflower
20 ml (¾ fl oz/1 tablespoon) tahini
60 g (2 oz/¼ cup) Greek yoghurt
squeeze of lemon juice
20 ml (¾ fl oz/1 tablespoon) water
40 g (1½ oz/¼ cup) pine nuts,
    roasted
60 g (2 oz/½ cup) dried
    cranberries
¼ cup coriander (cilantro) leaves
¼ cup flat-leaf parsley

Preheat oven to 220 °C (430 °F).

Rinse and pat dry the chickpeas, then place them in a roasting tray and season with half a teaspoon of salt and a tablespoon of the olive oil. Roast for 25 minutes, or until golden brown and crunchy. Remove, season with cumin powder and allow to cool.

The cauliflower for this salad is best cooked on a barbecue, however you can use a very hot chargrill pan instead. Remove the stem from the cauliflower and cut the head into large florets. Place the cauliflower into a large mixing bowl and toss with 2 tablespoons of olive oil and 1 teaspoon of salt. On the grill of your barbecue cook the cauliflower until slightly charred and tender to touch, being sure not to overcook the cauliflower so that it does not become soggy. Set aside on a serving platter.

In a medium mixing bowl thoroughly combine the tahini, yoghurt, lemon juice, water and the remaining salt. To finish, add the chickpeas to the serving platter, drizzle the tahini dressing over the top and garnish with pine nuts, dried cranberries, coriander (cilantro) and flat-leaf parsley.

FARMERS' MARKETS

Jimmy Shu

On a Sunday morning at the Darwin Rapid Creek markets you'll often see spectacled Jimmy Shu with a grin from ear to ear, prodding, sniffing and tasting the produce, and chatting to the stallholders. A renowned chef, and owner of the Hanuman restaurants, he has called Darwin home since the early '90s.

Jimmy first came to Darwin to source 'silver barramundi' for his restaurants back in Melbourne. He was met at the airport by a barefoot Billy Bousted—now his dearest friend—and was shown the local produce. What he found was a delicious array of South-East Asian herbs, vegetables and fruits that flourish in the tropical climate. He never went back to Melbourne.

When Jimmy initially opened Hanuman he was the chef, waiter, sommelier, cleaner and dishwasher. He worked seven days a

week from 7 am to midnight, as well as with walking the 4 kilometres and from work four times a day so that he could have a sleep between the lunch and dinner service.

With Jimmy's love for fresh, exotic produce and cuisine it wasn't long before Hanuman was an established name, not only in the Top End but throughout Australia. Jimmy now devotes his time to developing the local produce and farmers' markets around the Northern Territory.

EGGPLANT PACHADI

My friend Jimmy Shu possibly does the best eggplant pachadi I have ever tasted, but he will never pass on his recipe, so this is my version. However, Jimmy did tell me it is essential to use fresh tomato, crushed tinned tomato and tomato paste/puree. This is a rich dish, so some yoghurt sauce is great along with some steamed rice and/or roti.

6 Japanese eggplant, quartered lengthways
1 teaspoon table salt
1 teaspoon turmeric powder
4 tablespoons vegetable oil, for frying

FOR TOMATO SAUCE

1½ tablespoons olive oil
1 banana shallot, finely diced
1 garlic clove, finely chopped
1 teaspoon ginger, grated
1 teaspoon table salt
2 cardamon pods, bruised
1 teaspoon cumin powder
½ teaspoon cumin seeds
1 teaspoon coriander powder
½ teaspoon chilli flakes (optional, to taste)
½ teaspoon yellow mustard seeds
1 tablespoon tomato paste
250 g (9 oz/1 cup) crushed tinned tomatoes
2 fresh tomatoes, roughly chopped
2 sprigs curry leaves
3 teaspoons brown sugar

TO SERVE

½ cup coriander (cilantro) leaves
1 sprig curry leaves
yoghurt

Start by salting the eggplants and letting them drain in a colander in the sink for 20 minutes. Rinse and dry the eggplants with absorbent paper and set aside.

Heat the olive oil in a saucepan over medium–high heat and cook the shallots until translucent and tender, around 6–8 minutes. Add the garlic and ginger and cook for a further 1–2 minutes. Add the spices and salt and cook while stirring constantly for a further 2 minutes. Add the tomato paste and cook for 2–3 minutes before adding the tinned tomatoes, fresh tomatoes, fresh curry leaves and brown sugar. Reduce the heat to low and cook for 20–25 minutes to allow the flavours to develop. Blitz with a stick blender for 35–40 seconds after cooking. Check seasoning before serving.

Meanwhile heat the vegetable oil in a large frying pan over high heat. Dust the eggplants in the turmeric powder and shallow fry in batches until golden brown, around 2–3 minutes. Drain on absorbent paper.

Serve the eggplants in the tomato sauce while they are still hot. Garnish with coriander (cilantro) leaves and curry leaves. Serve with yoghurt on the side.

BRUSSELS NOT LIKE YOUR GRANDMA'S

After a shaky start to eating brussels sprouts during my childhood I have found a new love for these miniature cabbages. Whatever you do, don't boil them until they are brown and bitter. Treat them with love: finely shave them and make raw salads or a coleslaw from them.

600 g (1 lb 5 oz) brussels sprouts
1½ tablespoons olive oil
100 ml (3½ fl oz/⅓ cup) vegetable stock
15 g (½ oz) unsalted butter
½ garlic clove, finely chopped
pinch of table salt
1 tablespoon lemon juice
80 g (2¾ oz/½ cup) almonds, roasted and roughly chopped

Preheat oven to 200 °C (400 °F).

Cut 500 g of the brussels sprouts in half lengthways and place them with the olive oil in an ovenproof frying pan over medium–high heat and sauté for 3–4 minutes. Once the pan is hot and the brussels sprouts start to brown, pour in the vegetable stock, add the garlic and place in the oven for 6–8 minutes.

Carefully and thinly slice the remaining brussels sprouts from the top to the bottom, and discard the stems.

Remove the brussels sprouts from the oven. The pan will be very hot so you will have to use a tea towel. Place the pan back on the stove over medium–high heat and add the butter. Toss well to combine and season with salt.

Toss the raw brussels sprouts with the lemon juice and sprinkle with the roasted almonds over the top of the cooked brussels.

PUMPKIN BRAISED IN MEAD

SERVES 6—8

1.5 kg (3 lb 5 oz) jap or kent
    pumpkin (winter squash)
2 tablespoons olive oil
1 onion, finely diced
2 star anise
180 ml (6 fl oz/¾ cup) semi-sweet
    mead
500 ml (17 fl oz/2 cups) vegetable
    stock
1 teaspoon table salt
½ cup manchego cheese, grated

Preheat oven to 180 °C (350 °F).

Peel the pumpkin (winter squash), remove the seeds and cut into 4 cm (1½ in) cubes.

Heat a shallow casserole dish over a medium–high heat on the stovetop. Add the oil and when the oil is hot, sauté the onion with the star anise until caramelised and aromatic. After 5 minutes add the pumpkin and sauté for a further 2 minutes. Deglaze the pumpkin with the mead and reduce by half, add the stock and salt and bring to boil. Cover and place in the oven, and bake for 1 hour, or until pumpkin is tender when pierced with a fork or skewer.

When cooked, take the pumpkin out, evenly coat it with the manchego cheese and bake uncovered for a further 20 minutes, or until the cheese has melted and browned on the top.

PUMPKIN SOUP WITH CANDIED PEPITAS

When I make puree and soups I keep it quite simple: I want the final product to taste like the ingredient I want to showcase. For pumpkin (winter squash) soup I cook the pumpkin quickly to retain a freshness in the flavour and to ensure that the beautiful vibrant orange colour does not dull with overcooking.

PEPITAS

60 g (2 oz/⅓ cup) pepitas
  (pumpkin seeds)
1 tablespoon caster (superfine)
  sugar
1 teaspoon table salt

1 kg (2 lb 3 oz) butternut pumpkin
  (winter squash)
2 tablespoons olive oil
1½ teaspoons table salt
750 ml (25½ fl oz /3 cups) water
250 ml (8½ fl oz/1 cup) milk
50 g (1¾ oz) unsalted butter

To prepare the pepitas (pumpkin seeds), heat a frying pan over high heat and add the pepitas, sugar and salt. Don't move the pan for 1–2 minutes, until the sugar starts to melt. As the sugar melts, toss the pepitas in the pan until they are coated. Transfer to a lined baking tray and set aside to cool.

Peel the pumpkin (winter squash), remove the seeds and cut into 1 cm cubes. In a heavy-based pot that has a lid, heat the olive oil over high heat, add the pumpkin and the salt, and sauté for 2 minutes, stirring constantly. You want to slightly soften the pumpkin, however you do not want to brown it.

Add the water and bring to boil. Cover the pot and cook over a medium–high heat for 15–20 minutes, or until it is easily pierced with a fork.

When the pumpkin is cooked, add the milk and remove from the stove. Transfer the entire contents of the pot into a food processor. With the motor running add the butter and process on high for 2–3 minutes.

Once all the pumpkin has been processed, adjust the seasoning and/or consistency. If the soup is too thick add warm milk. If you want the soup thicker, return it to the stove and reduce over a medium heat until you have reached your desired consistency.

Serve the soup with the candied pepitas and grind white pepper over the top.

SEAFOOD

SEAFOOD

Fishing is a way of life in the Northern Territory, and I was fortunate enough to grow up on the famous Roper River, one of the Northern Territory's best fishing destinations. From a young age I fell in love with fishing. It wasn't easy though—my parents couldn't stand it—on rare occasions I would have to sneak off, without telling my parents, in the back of my uncles' Toyotas when they would go on fishing trips.

Fishing and camping by the river was always an incredible experience for me: not everyone gets the opportunity to catch and cook their own meal. I would spend hours fishing for the famed barramundi and sooty grunters, or wading in the shallows looking for yabbies and freshwater mussels. With no eskies and ice to take anything home, a strict catch-and-release rule was in place; this was a vital lesson at an early age about the importance of sensible, sustainable fishing. We would never take a fish for the sake of a catch. Any fish that we did keep for food was cooked immediately with nothing more than a wood fire, a wire rack and some salt. When you have a product that fresh there is nothing else you need.

Fishing, not dissimilar to farming, provides vital lessons on where our food comes from. When buying seafood it is imperative to source ethical and sustainable seafood. Our rivers and oceans have suffered from years of overfishing. By making the right choices at the fish markets you can positively influence the survival of our fishing industries.

The relatively untouched waters of the Top End coast and rivers have given rise to incredible seafood, which is sought after throughout Australia and the world. The Northern Territory has been a leader in sustainable fishing for many years and with much of the water being geographically protected—in other words, inaccessible—there is a natural barrier and protection for fish stocks.

In this chapter I use a lot of local produce found in the waters of the Top End, but these recipes are just a guide. You can substitute with your local produce if you cannot get your hands on what I use.

BANANA PRAWN POTS

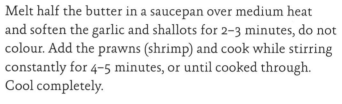

SERVES 8

I use banana prawns (shrimp) a lot because of their size and availability. Obviously, in the Top End we get some of Australia's freshest banana prawns, however, use any prawn that you like in this recipe, just use the same weight.

180 g (6½ oz) unsalted butter

2 garlic cloves, finely minced

1 tablespoon shallot, finely minced

300 g (10½ oz) raw banana prawns (shrimp), peeled and deveined

½ teaspoon sweet paprika

¼ teaspoon fresh nutmeg, grated

1 tablespoon capers

30 g (1 oz/1½ tablespoons) cornichons

3 tablespoons lemon juice

1½ teaspoons sea salt

1 tablespoon flat-leaf parsley, chopped

1½ tablespoon aioli (see page 20)

30 g (1 oz) cream cheese, at room temperature

Melt half the butter in a saucepan over medium heat and soften the garlic and shallots for 2–3 minutes, do not colour. Add the prawns (shrimp) and cook while stirring constantly for 4–5 minutes, or until cooked through. Cool completely.

Transfer cold prawn mixture along with paprika and nutmeg to a food processor and blitz on high for 1–2 minutes, until a smooth paste has formed.

Add remaining ingredients and pulse five or six times, or until everything is thoroughly incorporated. Check seasoning and divide mixture between two to three ramekins. Set aside.

Melt remaining butter until foaming, cool slightly and skim the surface to remove any white solids. Top each ramekin with the clarified butter, place them in refrigerator and cool completely before serving.

Serve with a fresh baguette, freshly cracked white pepper and extra virgin olive oil.

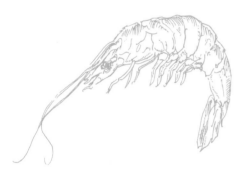

YABBY WITH PRESERVED CHILLI AND SESAME

These are little appetisers that I like to serve as something fun and different. If you cannot get yabby meat, scampi or banana prawn will do, picked crab meat will also work well in this recipe. Japanese mayonnaise goes with most things you eat, but feel free to use normal mayonnaise or aioli (see page 20) if you don't have any Japanese mayonnaise.

300 g (10½ oz) yabby meat,
   cooked and peeled
125 ml (4 fl oz/½ cup) Japanese
   mayonnaise
2 whole preserved chilli (see page
   14), finely diced
pinch freshly ground white pepper
3 teaspoons lemon juice
½ teaspoon freshly grated ginger
½ teaspoon sea salt

TO SERVE

5 sheets nori, cut into quarters
2 tablespoons bonito flakes
1 tablespoon black sesame seeds

Using a sharp knife finely dice the yabby meat into 3 mm chunks, alternatively you could pulse the yabby meat in the food processor until you reach the same consistency.

Place the chopped yabby meat into a mixing bowl, add the remaining ingredients and mix thoroughly. Check seasoning for acidity and salt.

Serve yabby meat mixture on nori squares, garnished with bonito flakes and sesame seeds.

PEARL MEAT SASHIMI

Pearl meat is such a delicate, subtle seafood. I eat it fresh and raw. If you don't go much for raw seafood, my mate Billy Bousted said you don't need to do much to it, just dust it in flour, pan sear it and serve it with lemon wedges. Fresh scallops make a good alternative to pearl meat in this recipe.

200 g (7 oz) fresh pearl meat
1 tablespoon curing salt (see page 9)
2 tablespoons olive oil
¼ teaspoon fresh ginger, finely grated
1 tablespoon finger lime pulp

In a plastic container completely cover the pearl meat with the curing salt, cover and place in the fridge for 30 minutes. After 30 minutes rinse the pearl meat with ice cold water and pat dry with paper towel.

Slice the pearl meat as thinly as possible on a bias. Place the sliced pearl meat into a small mixing bowl and add the olive oil and ginger. Toss the pearl meat until completely dressed.

Serve the pearl meat immediately on a plate to share, scattering the finger lime pulp over the meat.

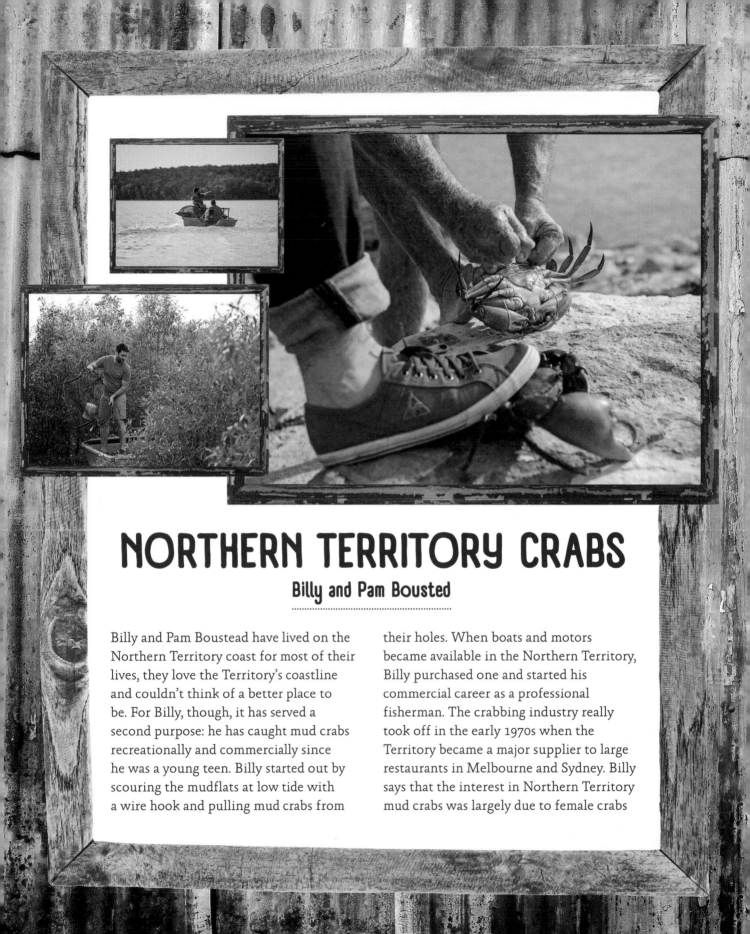

NORTHERN TERRITORY CRABS

Billy and Pam Bousted

Billy and Pam Boustead have lived on the Northern Territory coast for most of their lives, they love the Territory's coastline and couldn't think of a better place to be. For Billy, though, it has served a second purpose: he has caught mud crabs recreationally and commercially since he was a young teen. Billy started out by scouring the mudflats at low tide with a wire hook and pulling mud crabs from

their holes. When boats and motors became available in the Northern Territory, Billy purchased one and started his commercial career as a professional fisherman. The crabbing industry really took off in the early 1970s when the Territory became a major supplier to large restaurants in Melbourne and Sydney. Billy says that the interest in Northern Territory mud crabs was largely due to female crabs

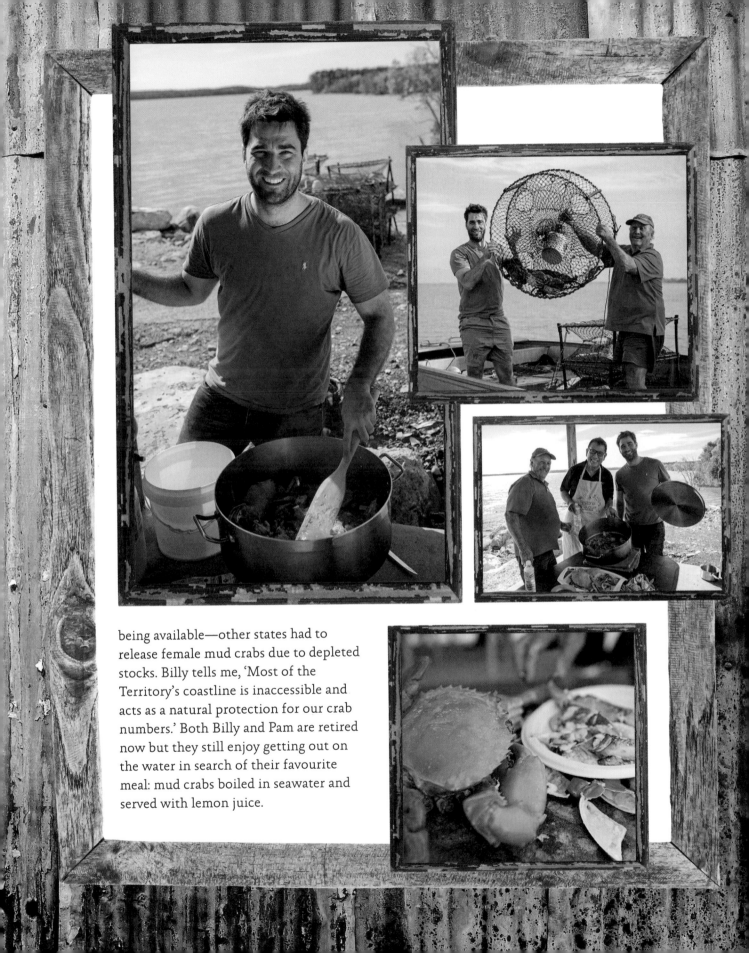

being available—other states had to release female mud crabs due to depleted stocks. Billy tells me, 'Most of the Territory's coastline is inaccessible and acts as a natural protection for our crab numbers.' Both Billy and Pam are retired now but they still enjoy getting out on the water in search of their favourite meal: mud crabs boiled in seawater and served with lemon juice.

TROPICAL LOBSTER WITH DASHI

SERVES 2

I enjoy cooking tropical lobsters on coals or the open flame of a barbecue, and this dish is definitely a crowd pleaser at any barbecue or dinner party. If you cannot get tropical rock lobsters, any crayfish will work in this recipe. You can buy nori powder at health food shops, otherwise blitz up sushi sheets in your spice grinder until you have a fine powder.

DASHI BUTTER

25 g (1 oz) unsalted butter, softened
1 teaspoon dashi powder
1 teaspoon nori powder

1 × 800 g (1 lb 12 oz) tropical rock lobster, split in half lengthways and stomach removed
1 tablespoon olive oil
1 teaspoon table salt
juice of ½ lemon
1 tablespoon chives, finely chopped

To start this dish prepare the dashi butter first because as you cook the lobster you will be basting it in the butter.

Place the ingredients for the dashi butter into a small bowl and combine thoroughly. Set aside with a pastry brush for basting the lobster while it cooks.

Preheat the grill on your barbecue to medium–high. Season each half of the lobster with the olive oil and salt, place the lobster halves flesh-side down first and cook for 6–7 minutes, or until charred. Turn the lobster so that the flesh-side is now up, apply the dashi butter with a pastry brush and cook for 10–12 minutes, or until the lobster is cooked through. Once the lobster is cooked, remove the halves from the barbecue, give a final (generous) brush of dashi butter, season with fresh lemon juice and garnish with chives. Serve immediately.

MUSSELS AND PEAS

SERVES 4

150 g (5½ oz) frozen peas

2 tablespoons cream

1 tablespoon olive oil

½ brown onion, finely diced

800 g (1 lb 12 oz) live mussels,
cleaned and debearded

125 ml (4 fl oz/½ cup) dry white
wine

125 ml (4 fl oz/½ cup) fish stock,
warmed and reduced by half

20 g (¾ oz) unsalted butter

2 tablespoons lemon juice

50 g (1¾ oz) pea shoots

1 teaspoon sea salt

TO SERVE

1 tablespoon extra virgin olive oil

warm sourdough bread

Start by making a pea puree. As the peas have been frozen there is no need to cook them to soften. Simply thaw the peas in hot water, transfer to a food processor and process on high for 3–4 minutes with the cream. Pass the pea puree through a sieve and set aside.

In a large sauté pan that has a lid heat the olive oil over medium heat and gently soften the onion. When the onion is translucent, add the mussels and toss to coat. Deglaze with the white wine and reduce for a minute. Add the stock, cover and cook the mussels for 2–3 minutes, or until the mussels have opened. Discard any that haven't opened. When the mussels have all opened, reduce the heat on the stove to low, add the butter, pea puree, lemon juice, pea shoots and salt, combine well. Adjust the seasoning before you serve the mussels.

Serve the mussels in a large bowl with extra virgin olive oil and warm bread to soak up the beautiful sauce.

CRAB COOKED IN SEAWATER WITH *NAM JIM*

SERVES 4–6

This is my go-to camping dish. Before I leave the house I make a big batch of *nam jim* (Thai dipping sauce) and pack a stockpot for boiling the crabs, and off I go. So simple, yet cooking the crabs in seawater really does give them an unreal taste. If you find yourself without seawater or a pot, cooking the mud crabs on open coals is a very easy variation which imparts a wonderful flavour. The *nam jim* in this recipe is a terrific sauce to have in the fridge, it's great on salads and is a prefect sauce for a lot of seafood. If you can't get mud crabs, blue swimmer crabs are a great alternative.

2 whole mud crabs

NAM JIM
100 ml (3½ fl oz/⅓ cup) lime juice
2 tablespoons fish sauce
60 g (2 oz/⅓ cup) palm sugar (jaggery), shaved
1 tablespoon coriander root
½ teaspoon garlic clove, chopped
½ red Thai chilli
2 tablespoons finely sliced lemongrass, white part only
1 tablespoon Thai basil stem
1 teaspoon galangal, grated ginger can be used if you cannot get galangal
pinch of table salt

Place all the ingredients for the *nam jim* in a food processor and process on high for 2 minutes, or until the sugar has dissolved and the ingredients are finely chopped. This sauce will last for one week in an airtight container in the fridge.

For the crabs, boil a large pot of seawater—enough to completely cover the mud crabs—and boil the crabs whole for 20–22 minutes, or until cooked through. They are cooked through when the shell turns bright orange and the flesh turns white. If you don't have seawater readily available, heavily salted water will do the job. When the crabs are cooked remove them from the boiling water and put straight into a salted ice bath to prevent overcooking. When the crabs have cooled, simply eat with the *nam jim*.

DARWIN FISH MARKET

Ziko and Carmel

You would be hard pressed to find anyone more passionate about sustainable, local seafood than Ziko and Carmel. Owners and operators of Darwin Fish Market, they have made it their mission to promote, support, stock and encourage restaurants, hotels and retailers to use Australian-only seafood. Ziko and Carmel stock 100 per cent Australian seafood and 98 per cent of

their product is proudly marked 'Northern Territory seafood'.

When they initially opened their business they were told that they would not survive if they didn't sell imported products. Carmel and Ziko stuck to their guns and have created a Territory icon, which they credit largely to being able to source beautiful produce from local waters.

Coining the phrase 'Go wild … Go Territory wild', they are a testament to sustainability.

Carmel is a member of Women In Seafood, which tackles policy within the Australian commercial seafood industry. Meanwhile, Ziko has played a key role in rallying support within the community for stricter labelling laws throughout Australia for local and imported seafood.

CHILLI MUD CRAB

SERVES 4

You do not have to use mud crabs for this recipe, whatever crab is local and sustainable from your fishmonger will work just as well. My friend Craig tells me blue swimmer crab is probably his next pick after the mud crab—with the amount of chilli and crabs this man has cooked I will take his word for it.

1 (1.2–1.5 kg/2 lb 10 oz–3 lb
    5 oz) whole mud crab, cleaned,
    quartered and claws cracked
1 tablespoon rice flour
2 ripe tomatoes, cut into chunks

SAUCE

60 ml (2 fl oz/¼ cup) vegetable oil
2 banana shallots, thinly sliced
4 garlic cloves, finely chopped
3 long red chillies, thinly sliced
2 Thai red chillies, thinly sliced
2 teaspoons ginger, grated
3 teaspoons belacan (shrimp paste)
80 ml (2½ fl oz/⅓ cup) rice wine
    vinegar
1¼ tablespoons caster (superfine)
    sugar
170 ml (5½ fl oz/⅔ cup) tinned
    crushed tomatoes
2 tablespoons fish sauce
1½ tablespoons soy sauce
250 ml (8½ fl oz/1 cup) water

TO SERVE

¼ cup coriander leaves (cilantro)
¼ cup spring onions (scallion),
    thinly sliced
¼ cup Thai basil

If you are preparing the crab yourself, save the liquid from the claws and add it to the sauce.

Heat the vegetable oil in a large wok or sauté pan over medium–high heat. Add the shallots, garlic, chillies and ginger and gently sauté for 3 minutes until the shallots start to brown and the garlic is aromatic. Add the belacan and sauté for a further minute. Add the vinegar, sugar and crushed tomatoes, soy sauce and water. Bring to boil, then reduce to a simmer and cook covered for 10–15 minutes.

Dust the mud crab with the rice flour and add to the sauce, along with the chopped ripe tomatoes. Simmer covered for 10–12 minutes, or until the crab is cooked through—when the flesh turns white and shell turns bright orange. Occasionally stir the mud crab to ensure even cooking and an even coating of sauce. When the crab is cooked, serve on a platter with the herbs scattered on top.

FISH BURGERS

You can use most types of white fish in this recipe. I frequently use barramundi or snapper. Feel free to give your favourite fish a go.

600 g (1 lb 5 oz) firm white fish,
   cut into 3 mm (⅛ in) cubes
2 tablespoons olive oil
60 g (2 oz/1 cup) panko (Japanese
   breadcrumbs)
grated zest of 1 lemon
½ cup flat-leaf parsley, finely
   chopped
2 teaspoons sweet paprika
2 teaspoons seeded mustard
1 teaspoon table salt
1 litre (34 fl oz/4 cups) vegetable
   oil

BATTER
150 g (5½ oz/1 cup) plain
   (all-purpose) flour
90 g (3 oz/½ cup) rice flour
3 teaspoons table salt
375 ml (12½ fl oz/1½ cups) cold
   soda water

TO SERVE
6 burger buns of your choosing
butter lettuce, rinsed and dried
125 ml (4 fl oz/½ cup) aioli
   (see page 20)
freshly ground white pepper

In a large mixing bowl combine the ingredients for the burger and mix thoroughly with a wooden spoon. It is important to really work the burger mixture with the back of the wooden spoon against the mixing bowl, this will help bind the patties and make it easier to handle and cook.

Divide the burger mixture into six and form six patties. Firmly squeeze the patties to bind them. Place the fish patties on a lined tray and refrigerate for an hour before cooking.

Preheat the oil in a deep sauté pan to 180 °C (350 °F). If you don't have a thermometer, the oil is ready to use when a piece of bread fries to golden brown in 20 seconds.

Meanwhile make the batter. Combine the ingredients using a fork in a medium-sized mixing bowl. Do not over-mix the batter and it is important to only use a fork. The consistency of the batter should be like pancake batter. Lumps in the mix are fine.

Dip the fish patties in the batter and fry in batches for 6–8 minutes. The burgers should be completely submerged in oil. You may have to add more oil if the burgers are not completely covered when dropped into the oil. Drain the patties on paper towel to absorb excess oil.

To assemble the burgers, spread the aioli on the buns, place the lettuce on top, then the patties, and sprinkle with the white pepper. I like my burger fillings simple, however you can put anything you like on these fish burgers.

STEVE'S SALMON POACHED IN COCONUT

SERVES 4

4 × 200–250 g (7 oz–9 oz)
   salmon fillets, skin off
1 teaspoon table salt

SAUCE

1 tablespoon peanut oil
2 purple shallots
2 teaspoons ground coriander
400 ml (13½ fl oz /1⅔ cups)
   coconut milk
200 ml (7 fl oz/¾ cup) fish stock,
   warmed and reduced by half
2 long red chilli, sliced thinly
1 stick lemon grass, white part
   only and thinly sliced
50 g (1¾ oz/¼ cup) palm sugar
   (jaggery)
2 tablespoons fish sauce
1 teaspoon ginger, grated
3 kaffir lime leaves

TO SERVE

¼ cup coriander (cilantro) leaves
¼ cup Thai basil leaves
2 tablespoons fried shallots

Heat the peanut oil in a large non-stick pan over medium–high heat. Add the shallots and brown for 3–4 minutes. Add the ground coriander and cook until fragrant, around 40–60 seconds. Add the remaining ingredients for the sauce, bring to boil, then reduce the heat to a gentle simmer and cook sauce for 15 minutes, until all the flavours have released into the coconut milk.

Season the salmon fillets with salt and place into coconut sauce. Gently poach for 10–12 minutes, or until the fillets are cooked. Serve the salmon with the sauce and a scattering of the herbs and fried shallots.

HUMPTY DOO BARRAMUNDI
Bob and Dan Richards

Situated between Darwin and Kakadu National Park lies the family-run business Humpty Doo Barramundi. This secluded farm is an understated industry leader: Humpty Doo Barra supplies a fifth of Australia's barramundi on a weekly basis, every week of the year.

Bob and Dan—the father and son duo who are third and fourth generation Territorians—have been leaders in sustainable aquaculture in Australia for many years. Bob is widely recognised for his efforts within sustainable aquaculture, and received the Churchill Fellowship in 2002 to bring knowledge from aquaculture around the world back to the Australian industry.

The Humpty Doo farm started off with nothing but two small saltwater ponds in the middle of nowhere, with no road access, no power and no toilets. They have had an annual growth rate of over

30 per cent for the last fifteen years and production has grown from around 300 kilograms annually to well over a 1000 tonnes of barramundi annually at present. Only four years ago they employed three staff, now it is over twenty-two. They are the biggest Barramundi producer in Australia.

Bob and Dan travel the world to learn cutting-edge technology and techniques but they have also been pioneers in developing world-first on-farm technology within the aquaculture industry. One of Bob's inventions is an audio-activated feeding system, which has drastically reduced wastage and maximised efficiency.

Along with their tenacious attitude and ingenious production methods, the Richards also credit their product quality to the pristine saltwater of the Adelaide River, giving their fish the distinctive chrome colour associated with saltwater barramundi, along with their clean saltwater taste.

The Richards family send their product all over Australia and have also sent it internationally for special events. Humpty Doo Barramundi products have graced the tables of many high profile restaurants and it's a sought after product for high-end retailers throughout Australia.

WHOLE BAKED BARRAMUNDI WITH POMELO

SERVES 4

I originally cooked the fish in paperbark in Kakadu and made the dressing with what ingredients I had lying around. I have since tailored it a little and use the dressing all the time. Sometimes I serve roasted sweet potato in wattle seed with this dish and it works great — sounds funny but it's a great match.

1–1.5 kg (2 lb 7 oz–3 lb 5 oz) barramundi, cleaned
2½ teaspoons sea salt
2 tablespoons olive oil
150 g (5½ oz) pomelo (Chinese grapefruit), picked flesh

DRESSING

½ teaspoon ginger, grated
2 teaspoons purple shallot, finely chopped
½ garlic clove
1½ tablespoons Thai basil leaves, finely chopped
4 tablespoons olive oil
1½ tablespoons lemon juice

TO SERVE

½ cup Thai basil leaves
½ cup coriander (cilantro) leaves

Preheat oven to 200 °C (400 °F).

Line a baking tray with ovenproof paper. Season the barramundi with 2 teaspoons of the salt and the olive oil Be sure to season the cavity of the barramundi. Bake the barramundi for 20–25 minutes, or until the flesh behind the head is cooked and flakes from the bone easily.

Meanwhile make the dressing. In a mortar and pestle grind the ginger, shallot, garlic, remaining half a teaspoon of salt, basil leaves and olive oil to a fine paste. Add the lemon juice and check the seasoning.

Place the whole fish carefully on a serving dish, spoon over the dressing and scatter with the pomelo (Chinese grapefruit), Thai basil and coriander (cilantro) leaves.

SEARED MACKEREL AND TOMATOES

SERVES 4

This dish is best through the summer months
when tomatoes are at their peak.

4 × 200 g (7 oz) mackerel fillets,
    skin off
3 tablespoons olive oil
1 teaspoon sea salt
2 small heirloom tomatoes
2 large ox-heart tomatoes
80 g (2¾ oz) kalamata olives,
    torn into rough pieces
2 tablespoons tarragon leaves
lemon vinaigrette (see page 20),
    to serve

Preheat a chargrill pan over high heat and season
the mackerel with the olive oil and salt. Seal the
mackerel fillets quickly on all sides until seared and
slightly charred, approximately 3–4 minutes. You do
not want to cook the mackerel fillets all the way
through. Rest the fillets for 5 minutes before slicing
into 1 cm thick pieces.

Slice the tomatoes as thinly as possible. I use a very
sharp knife, however a mandoline can make the job
easier if you don't trust your knife skills. Try to keep
the slices whole for presentation.

Once the tomatoes are sliced, drape them evenly
between the plates making sure to have a mix of all
the varieties on each plate. Lay the sliced mackerel
on the tomatoes, scatter with the torn olives and
dress the mackerel and tomatoes with the lemon
vinaigrette and tarragon leaves. Serve immediately.

GOLD BAND SNAPPER

SERVES 4

Gold band snapper is a beautiful local fish from the Northern Territory. It's as versatile as it is easy to cook. Throw it on the barbecue, cook it in a pan or roast it. Kingfish or normal snapper are good alternatives to gold band snapper.

6 small banana shallots, peeled and cut in half lengthways
60 ml (2 fl oz/¼ cup) soy sauce
1 tablespoon umeboshi vinegar
1 tablespoon mirin
3 tablespoons vegetable oil
4 × 200 g (7 oz) snapper, skin on
1½ teaspoons table salt
150 g (5½ oz) snow peas (mangetout), finely julienned
1 red capsicum, membrane removed and finely julienned
1 tablespoon lemon vinaigrette (see page 20)

Preheat oven to 160 °C (320 °F).

In a roasting tray place shallots, soy sauce, umeboshi vinegar and mirin, and roast uncovered, turning once, for 16–18 minutes, or until shallots are tender. Remove shallots once cooked, reserving 2 tablespoons of the cooking liquid for use in the dressing.

Meanwhile heat the vegetable oil in a large non-stick frying pan over high heat. Season the snapper fillets well with the salt and place skin-side down into the hot pan. Reduce the pan to a medium–high heat after a minute and cook the fillets for a further 4–5 minutes on the skin side, or until almost cooked through. Turn the fillets and finish for the last minute skin-side up. Place on paper towel and let rest for 2–3 minutes.

As the fish is resting, make the capsicum and snow pea (mangetout) salad. Combine the julienned snow peas and capsicum in a small mixing bowl, add the reserved cooking liquid from the shallots and lemon vinaigrette, and toss well to combine.

To serve, spoon the shallots onto the centre of six plates. Place the capsicum and snow pea salad on top of the shallots, and the snapper fillets on top of this salad-shallot mixture. Serve immediately.

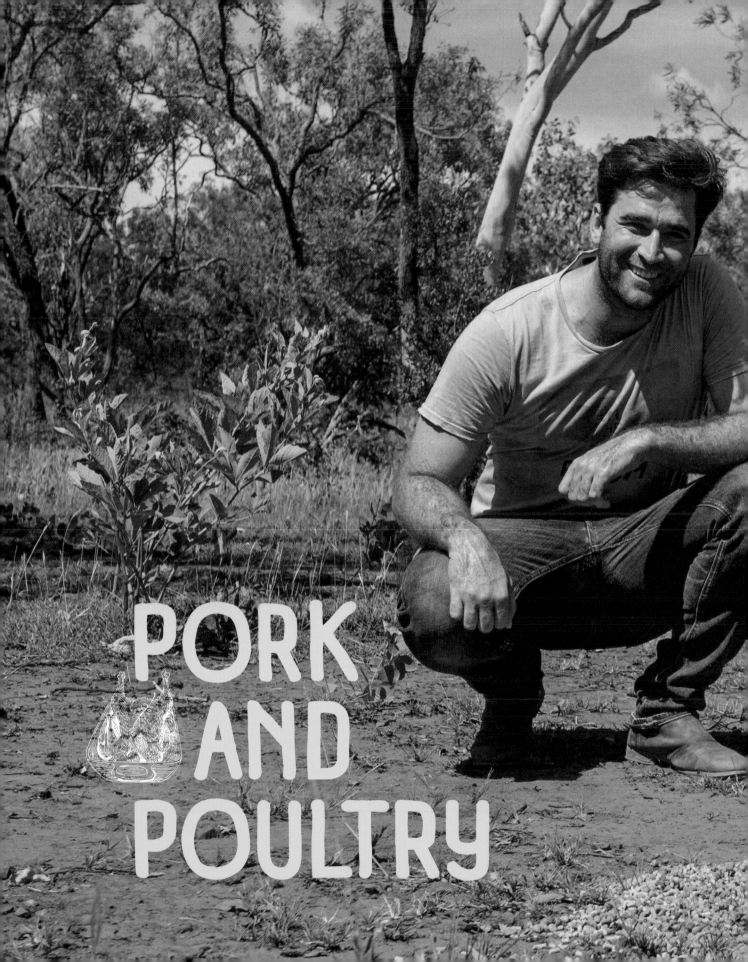

PORK
AND
POULTRY

PORK
AND
POULTRY

Without lecturing and getting high and mighty, always choose organic, hormone free, free-range pork, poultry and eggs. Really do your research and don't be fooled by big marketing tactics. By choosing these products you will help to create more ethical farming practices and contribute to advancements in sustainability in the agricultural industry.

Rural Australia has always put a big emphasis on domestic chickens and pigs. The benefits are threefold: they are a valuable source of meat; chickens produce eggs; and both pigs and chickens are fed scraps from the kitchen, which reduces waste and keeps the cost of raising the animals to an absolute minimum. Growing up, we always had domesticated chickens and pigs on our properties, and always in close proximity to us. Having to slaughter these animals from a young age taught me the realities of eating meat and the importance of ethically farmed and produced livestock.

In the Northern Territory there aren't facilities for commercial pork and poultry farming. Instead there are a large number of private farmers and breeders. Due to the fact that the breeders in the Northern Territory aren't commercial, they are purveyors of the less common and, quite often, heritage breeds of pork and poultry.

The most common pig breeds within the Northern Territory are the Tamworth, the Landrace and the Large White, however everyone has their favourite lesser known breed. A friend of mine who is an avid private pig farmer has his own unique breed, which has even been crossbred at one stage with wild pig bloodlines of the Northern Territory—it is said that the wild pigs of the Northern Territory are descendants of domestic pigs with a mixture of bloodlines ranging from Timor to India to the UK. The famed Berkshire pig is one of the most dominant bloodlines in the wild pigs of the Northern Territory, so he is probably not exaggerating when he says it gives his pigs a better taste.

Poultry isn't limited to the humble and highly valued chicken. Breeds found in the Territory range from geese to turkeys, guinea fowl to ducks. Not all are raised for meat consumption, with many being used for their eggs. Poultry breeders within the Northern Territory take it upon themselves to preserve and ensure the survival of less common and heritage breeds.

SICHUAN FRIED CHICKEN RIBS

1 kg (2 lb 3 oz) chicken ribs
2 star anise
½ stick cinnamon
2 teaspoons fennel seeds
4 allspice berries
2 teaspoons table salt
500 ml (17 fl oz/2 cups) chicken
  stock
4 spring onions (scallion)
1 litre (34 fl oz/4 cups) vegetable
  oil, for frying
60 ml (2 fl oz/¼ cup) aioli
  (see page 20), to serve

DUSTING
175 g (6 oz/1 cup) rice flour
2 teaspoons table salt
3 tablespoons Sichuan pepper,
  ground

Preheat oven to 160 °C (320 °F).

In a deep baking tray combine the chicken ribs with the spices, salt, stock and spring onions (scallion). Cover in foil and bake for 2 hours, or until the ribs are tender and the meat comes away from the bone easily. Remove the chicken ribs from the oven and let them cool completely in the cooking liquid. Remove the ribs from the cooking liquid and place them on a tray lined with paper towel to absorb excess liquid.

Heat the oil in a deep pot to 170 °C (340 °F). If you don't have a thermometer, the oil is ready when a piece of bread fries to golden brown in 20 seconds.

Meanwhile, combine the rice flour, salt and Sichuan pepper in a large baking tray. When the oil is ready, coat the chicken ribs with the Sichuan flour and fry in batches until golden brown and crispy, around 3–4 minutes per batch. When they are cooked, remove the chicken ribs with a slotted spoon and drain on paper towel. Let the oil reheat after each batch.

Serve immediately with the aioli.

PULL-APART CHICKEN

If you are going to make this recipe I would definitely recommend making extra — it's great in a chicken roll the next day with fresh coriander, chilli and some aioli (see page 20).

1 kg (2 lb 3 oz) chicken thighs, skin off
2 tablespoons vegetable oil
1½ teaspoons table salt
80 ml (2½ fl oz/⅓ cup) curry paste
150 g (5½ oz/1 cup) cashew nuts, roasted and finely chopped
190 ml (6½ fl oz/¾ cup) chicken stock
3 tablespoons coconut cream

TO SERVE

juice of 1 lime
½ cup coriander (cilantro), freshly picked
2 long red chillies, thinly sliced
steamed rice

Preheat your oven to 150 °C (300 °F).

Heat a heavy-based casserole dish, which has a lid, over high heat on your stove. Season the chicken thighs with the oil and salt, and seal them in batches until they are golden brown, this will take 3–4 minutes per batch. Do not overcrowd the casserole dish. Let the dish heat up again after each batch is cooked.

Once all the chicken thighs have been sealed, place them all back into the casserole dish along with the curry paste and chopped cashews. Cook for 3–4 minutes, or until the curry paste is fragrant and starts to catch on the bottom of the casserole dish. Add the chicken stock, cover the dish and bake in the oven for 2½ hours, or until the chicken is tender and falls apart.

Remove the dish from the oven and stir through the coconut cream. Increase the temperature of your oven to 190 °C (375 °F) and cook for a further 30 minutes, or until most of the liquid has evaporated and you are left with a thick sauce.

Remove the dish from the oven. Allow to cool slightly before squeezing the fresh lime juice over the top and garnishing with fresh coriander (cilantro) and chilli.

CHICKEN IN A KETTLE BBQ

SERVES 6

Cooking on a kettle BBQ transfers such a beautiful flavour to meat and vegetables. If you don't have a kettle BBQ you can cook the chicken in an oven, simply cook it like you would any other roast chicken. I do not stuff the chicken, instead I only cut a lemon into three and sit that in the cavity so that the flavour can be absorbed completely throughout the cooking.

1 large chicken, wishbone removed
1 lemon
½ tablespoon table salt

HERB BUTTER

60 g (2 oz) unsalted butter
40 g (1½ oz/⅔ cup) panko
 (Japanese breadcrumbs)
2 teaspoons seeded mustard
2 teaspoons fresh oregano
2 teaspoons fresh thyme
1 teaspoon fresh rosemary
½ teaspoon chilli flakes
1 teaspoon table salt

Prepare your kettle BBQ for medium indirect heat. If you have a thermometer, somewhere between 150–170 °C (300–340 °F); 160 °C (320 °F) is the optimum temperature.

In a food processor blend all the herb butter ingredients on high for 2–3 minutes, until everything is incorporated.

Before the butter can be placed under the skin you must first separate the skin from the breast meat. Using clean hands, gently insert your hand between the breast and the skin from the neck end of the chicken, continue to work your hand all over the breast meat, keeping it as flat as possible so that you do not tear the skin. Once the skin is free of the breast meat but still intact it is ready to be stuffed with the herb butter.

Using two-thirds of the herb butter, gently massage it over the breast meat under the skin. The more area the butter covers the better the end result will be.

Cut the lemon into thirds and insert it into the cavity of the chicken, season with the salt, rub remaining butter on top of the chicken, place the whole chicken into a baking tray breast-side up and cook for 2 hours. You may have to add more coals to your kettle BBQ throughout the cooking time so that the temperature doesn't drop too low.

Once the chicken has finished cooking, remove it from the kettle BBQ and cover it in aluminium foil for 20 minutes to rest. Carve the chicken, spoon over the melted butter and squeeze the cooked lemons over the cut meat before serving.

DUCK BREAST WITH BLOOD ORANGE AND FENNEL

SERVES 4

1½ large fennel bulbs, stems
    removed and bulbs halved
2 teaspoons lemon juice
1 teaspoon table salt
20 g (¾ oz) unsalted butter
2 tablespoons cream
4 duck breasts, skin scored
1 blood orange, segmented
1 tablespoon extra virgin olive oil
fennel fronds to garnish
½ red radicchio, leaves separated
    and trimmed

DRESSING

2 teaspoons sherry vinegar
1½ tablespoons blood orange juice
2 teaspoons maple syrup
1½ tablespoons extra virgin
    olive oil
½ teaspoon sea salt

Preheat oven to 180 °C (350 °F).

To start, make the fennel puree. Toss the fennel bulb halves in the fresh lemon juice and steam in a steamer over high heat for 20 minutes, or until completely soft when pierced with a knife.

When the fennel is cooked, transfer it to a food processor bowl and process on high. With the motor running add half a teaspoon of salt, the butter and cream. Process for 3–4 minutes, scraping the sides occasionally. Pass fennel puree through a fine sieve and set aside in a small pot with a lid, ready to reheat when the duck is cooked.

Season the skin of the duck breasts with the remaining salt. Place the duck breasts skin-side down in a large, cold ovenproof frying pan. Heat the pan over high heat with the duck in it, rendering the fat until the skin starts to turn golden, approximately 5 minutes. Without turning the duck, put the pan into the oven and roast for 3 minutes. Open the oven and using a tea towel remove the pan and turn the duck, cook the duck for a further 3 minutes, skin-side up. Remove the duck breast and rest it for 5–6 minutes.

Meanwhile, make the blood orange dressing by combining all the ingredients in a small mixing bowl with a whisk.

To serve, warm the puree gently and spoon onto a plate, slice the duck breast in half lengthways and give two halves per person, spoon the blood orange dressing over the cut duck breast and garnish with blood orange segments, fennel fronds and radicchio leaves dressed in extra virgin olive oil.

PIG FARMERS

Stu 'Bigfoot' Beckett & Chris 'Yatesy' Yates

Commercial pig farms don't operate in the Northern Territory, so backyard breeding has taken off to supply the locals with quality pork. In the backyard farms you will find predominately Large White, Landrace and Duroc breeds. Everyone has their favourite, depending on if they prefer bacon, pork or ham. As a backyard pig breeder you can't sell pork products to the public, however you can give it to your friends and family free of charge. This law has led to a very generous community of pig breeders who love to share their product with everyone.

This type of generosity is exactly what Stu and Chris love about backyard pig breeding. With over twenty years' experience between them, they have got breeding and raising pigs down to an exact science ... well almost.

When they initially started breeding in the Territory, one of the first things they realised was that most of the pig

population was line-bred because the community of breeders was quite small and they all shared breeding pigs with one another. Stu buys stud pigs from interstate and brings them up to the Northern Territory to introduce new bloodlines and breed better meat producing animals. At the moment the pride of Stu and Chris's stud is a prime example of impressive bloodlines: a Duroc, Leonard is a 300-plus kilogram monster of a pig that towers to 2.5 metres tall when he stands on his hind legs at feeding time. The Duroc is a crossbreed between the famous breeds of pig, the Tamworth and the Berkshire, and he was specifically bred for the Australian climate.

All of the pigs raised by Stu and Chris in their backyard pig farm are free to roam throughout the property, enjoying a peaceful life living off natural pasture and, in the dry season, specially formulated pig feed. This is important to Stu and Chris because they know exactly how their pigs are treated and exactly what they have eaten throughout their life. In a time when so much importance is put on where your meat comes from and how it is treated, Stu and Chris take pride in how their pigs are raised.

QUAIL WITH LEMON AND HONEY

SERVES 4 AS A STARTER

To have tender juicy quail, I brine mine overnight before cooking. This ensures that the quail is very forgiving in the cooking process and if you overcook the tricky bird it won't be as dry as the boot you grow plants in from your garden.

4 whole jumbo quails, quartered
2 tablespoons vegetable oil
3 tablespoons honey
4 lemon quarters, to serve

BRINE

70 g (2½ oz) table salt
1 tablespoon brown sugar
3 star anise
1 stick cinnamon
2.5 litres (85 fl oz/10 cups)
   cold water

SEASONING SALT

½ teaspoon ground cinnamon
½ teaspoon ground star anise
½ teaspoon ground Sichuan
   pepper
1 teaspoon ground fennel seeds
½ teaspoon ground cloves
1 teaspoon table salt

Combine the ingredients for the brine in a plastic container that will hold all the liquid plus the four quails. Stir the water to dissolve the sugar and salt, place the quails into the brine and refrigerate overnight.

Remove the quails and pat dry, discard brine. Mix the ingredients for the seasoning salt thoroughly in a small bowl.

Preheat a chargrill pan over medium–high heat. Season the quail generously with the seasoning salt and all the vegetable oil. Reserve a third of the seasoning salt for a final sprinkle after cooking.

Cook the quartered quails for 6–8 minutes each, or until cooked through, turning occasionally. In the final couple of minutes brush on the honey with a pastry brush.

Rest the quail for 5 minutes when it has finished cooking. Give a final sprinkle of the seasoning salt and serve with fresh lemon quarters.

PULLED PORK AND KOHLRABI SLIDERS

SERVES 8

Achiote paste is a special blend of spices that is used a lot in Mexican cuisine.
If you can't find achiote paste, tomato paste will work in the recipe also.

3 tablespoons vegetable oil

1 kg (2 lb 3 oz) pork shoulder, skin off, cut into 3–4 cm cubes

2 brown onions, finely chopped

40 g (1½ oz) achiote paste

2½ teaspoons table salt

2 teaspoons smoked paprika

2 star anise

4 allspice berries

2 teaspoons fennel seeds

½ tablespoon coffee powder

150 ml (5 fl oz/½ cup) apple cider

500 ml (17 fl oz/2 cups) veal stock

1¼ tablespoons brown sugar

40 ml (1¼ fl oz/2 tablespoons) red wine vinegar

3 bay leaves

KOHLRABI SALAD

1 cup finely shredded jicoma, if you cannot find jicoma replace it with daikon or extra kohlrabi

2 cups kohlrabi, finely shredded

40 ml (1¼ fl oz/2 tablespoons) fresh lemon juice

½ teaspoon sea salt

TO SERVE

8 brioche buns, cut in half

150 ml (5 fl oz/½ cup) aioli (see page 20)

Preheat oven to 140 °C (275 °F).

On the stove, heat the vegetable oil in a casserole dish over medium–high heat. Season the pork and brown in the casserole dish. Do this in three batches to avoid overcrowding, 6–7 minutes per batch. Don't be afraid to really cook the pork—it should be a deep brown.

Once browned, place the pork on paper towel. In the same pot and without draining off the oil, caramelise the onion. Once again, like the pork, brown the onion deeply but don't burn it, this will take 7–8 minutes. Return the pork to the dish.

Add the achiote paste along with the spices and coffee powder and cook for 1 minute, until aromatic. Deglaze the pot with the apple cider and reduce by half. Add the stock, sugar, vinegar and bay leaves and bring to boil. Cover the dish with the lid and place in the oven. Cook for 3 hours, or until the pork is tender and pulls apart easily.

Remove the pork from the oven and let it cool slightly in the cooking liquid before straining the liquid and reserving it in a large saucepan. Reduce the cooking liquid over high heat until reduced by a two-thirds to half, skimming the fat off as you go.

Meanwhile, shred the pork shoulder into a large container. Remove the allspice berries, cinnamon stick and bay leaves as you go. Pour the reduced liquid over the shredded pork.

To make the kohlrabi salad combine the jicoma, kohlrabi, lemon juice and salt in a medium mixing bowl and toss well.

To assemble the brioche buns, dollop a good amount of aioli on the base of each bun, spoon the pork between the buns evenly and top with the kohlrabi salad. Enjoy!

THE CRACKLING LOVER'S PORK BELLY

SERVES 6

1.5 kg (3 lb 5 oz) pork belly
300 g (10½ oz/1 cup) table salt
2 tablespoons fennel seeds
1 tablespoon caraway seeds

Start this recipe the day before you plan to cook the pork belly. Place the pork belly in a tray that will fit in your fridge. Combine the salt, fennel and caraway seeds, and completely cover the skin of the belly with the mix. Try not to let the salt fall off the skin and touch the flesh. Carefully place the tray in the bottom of your fridge. Leave it uncovered overnight.

Preheat oven to 220 °C (430 °F).

Remove the pork belly from the fridge and scrape as much of the salt off as you can with the back of a knife. Don't be overly worried if you cannot get all the salt off because this will act as the seasoning throughout the cooking process.

Place the pork belly in a baking tray and put it in the oven uncovered and cook it for 50 minutes at 220 °C (430 °F). Depending on your oven you may have to rotate the tray in the oven to avoid burning the belly. After 50 minutes reduce the temperature of the oven to 130 °C (266 °F) and cook for a further 2 hours.

Turn the oven off and let the pork rest for 30 minutes in the oven. Remove the pork from the oven, carve and serve immediately with your choice of sides.

PORK JOWL WITH CAULIFLOWER AND CURRY

3 pork jowls, skin on and gland
  removed (the butcher will
  do this)
250 g (9 oz/1 cup) table salt
50 g (1¾ oz/¼ cup) caster
  (superfine) sugar
3 teaspoons ground star anise

CAULIFLOWER PUREE

1½ tablespoons vegetable oil
¼ cauliflower, finely chopped
500 ml (17 fl oz/2 cups) water
2 tablespoons full cream
10 g (¼ oz) unsalted butter
½ teaspoon table salt

CURRANT JAM

80 ml (2½ fl oz/⅓ cup) verjuice
100 g (3½ oz/⅔ cup) currants

FOR THE CURRY SPICE

2 teaspoons ground fennel
1 teaspoon cumin
1 teaspoon salt
2 teaspoons brown sugar

TO SERVE

½ cup fried curry leaves
brown sauce (see page 25),
  optional

Start this recipe a day in advance. Place the jowls on a tray that will fit in your fridge. Combine the salt, sugar and star anise powder and generously cover the skin of each jowl. Try not to let the salt touch any flesh of the jowls. Pop the tray uncovered into the bottom of your fridge for 24 hours.

On the next day, preheat oven to 220 °C (430 °F). Scrape as much of the salt from the pork jowls as you can with the back of a knife. Place the pork into a roasting tray so that the jowls are not touching and cook in the oven for 50 minutes, you may have to rotate your roasting tray to prevent burning.

Turn the oven off. Without opening the door leave the pork in the oven for 2 hours. Remove, portion and serve the jowl.

Prepare the cauliflower puree. In a large non-stick frying pan heat the vegetable oil over medium–high heat. Add the cauliflower and salt. Sauté for 6–8 minutes, until the cauliflower becomes translucent. Deglaze the pan with the water and bring to boil. Cook the cauliflower for a further 12–14 minutes, or until the water has completely evaporated and the cauliflower is soft. Transfer it to a food processor and blend on high for 3–4 minutes. With the motor running add the cream and butter. Check seasoning and pass through a fine sieve into a small pot to keep warm for serving.

For the currant jam, combine the verjuice with the currants in a small pot over medium–high heat and bring to boil. Cook for 8–10 minutes, until the verjuice has reduced to almost nothing. Blend the currant puree in a food processor on high for 2–3 minutes, then pass through a fine sieve and set aside for serving.

Serve half a jowl to each person, along with cauliflower puree and currant jam. Mix the curry spice ingredients in a small bowl. Garnish the jowls with the curry spice, fried curry leaves and brown sauce.

MAKIN' BACON ... 'GREEN BACON'

Making your own bacon is great to do in the lead-up to a long weekend when all your friends and family gather for a nice time and there are plenty of morning fry-ups. Best of all; you can cut your bacon as thick or as thin as you want. Because you cure the bacon for a few days, it's great if you have a drinks fridge where it can sit uncovered without getting in the way of anything else. Just cast your eye over it every couple of days to make sure the liquid from the curing process doesn't overflow the container.

1.5 kg (3 lb 5 oz) pork belly, skin removed

CURE
300 g (10½ oz/1 cup) table salt
200 g (7 oz/1 cup) brown sugar
2 teaspoons ground cinnamon
1 tablespoon coriander seeds, ground
1 tablespoon juniper berries, ground
1 tablespoon fennel seeds, ground
2 teaspoons freshly ground black pepper

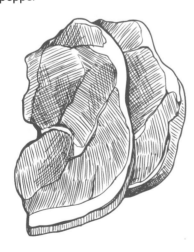

To cure your bacon you will ideally need a plastic container or stainless steel tray that is at least an inch bigger in all directions than the bacon. I suggest plastic or stainless steel so that the container doesn't react to the cure mix throughout the curing process.

Combine the curing ingredients thoroughly in a separate container before applying to the pork belly. Place the pork belly in a suitable container fat-side up and completely cover the belly in all of the cure mix. Place the pork belly in the bottom of your fridge uncovered for four days, turning the pork on the second day.

On the fourth day remove the pork belly from the cure mix. Rinse thoroughly under cold water and pat dry with absorbent paper. Leave uncovered in the fridge for a day to dry out before using, or covering and storing.

Slice and cook as needed. This bacon will last a week in the fridge. It freezes well and will last a couple of months frozen.

If you have a hot smoker you can hot smoke your bacon until the internal temperature reaches 160 °C (320 °F).

MEAT, DAIRY AND GAME

MEAT, DAIRY AND GAME

When you think of the meat and livestock industry of the Northern Territory your first—and most likely only—thought would be of the exotic Brahman cattle and the vast stations that span for thousands of square kilometres, where they roam. However, in recent years the farmers of the Territory have been diversifying and looking to different business models and ideas to suit the ever changing agricultural industry.

Small farms dotted around the Top End have begun to breed Damara sheep. Damara originate from East Asia and Egypt and more closely resemble a goat than a sheep. The taste of the Damara is almost identical to lamb, and if you ask a Damara farmer they'll tell you they prefer the taste of Damara meat over the more common breeds found in the southern states. Damara sheep are less susceptible to disease and more suitable to the warmer, wetter climate. Although they are becoming more common in the Top End, for now they are just supporting the demands of the local community.

Game meat consumption is on the rise in Australia, and with the Territory being home to nearly every species of game meat in Australia it has become an important supplier of these meats throughout the country and internationally. More farmers are turning to the farming of game meat. There are successful businesses operating crocodile farms in Darwin, wild camel properties in the Red Centre, kangaroo harvesters on the tablelands and buffalo stations in Arnhem Land.

One of my favourite examples of the diverse range of farms in the Territory would be a riverine buffalo dairy based in Litchfield—it is possibly one of the only buffalo dairies in the world to be based in a semi-arid environment. All these examples are a testament to the farmers of the Territory—and indeed Australia-wide—and their innovative plans to continue to adapt and grow their businesses to suit the conditions.

RICOTTA

MAKES APPROXIMATELY 300–350 G

Making your own ricotta cheese is very simple. I don't season my ricotta through the cooking process, so it can easily be used in both sweet and savoury dishes, which makes it a wonderfully versatile ingredient. As with most of my recipes, this ricotta recipe is more about the technique: I encourage you to try different types of milk. I love buffalo milk, it is such a rich, beautiful product. However, I also make ricotta from goat's milk or sheep's milk — pretty much if you have a favourite full-cream (whole) milk you can substitute it into this recipe. Enjoy showing off to your friends with this one. You will need a thermometer to make ricotta and if you are going to make ricotta often I would suggest buying ricotta baskets from a cheese supply store. However, some muslin (cheesecloth) and a colander will do the trick initially.

2 litres (68 fl oz/8 cups) full-cream (whole) buffalo milk
60 ml (2 fl oz/¼ cup) white wine vinegar

In a large saucepan over medium heat start to heat the buffalo milk to 94 °C (201 °F), stirring constantly to achieve even heating and avoid sticking.

While the milk is heating up prepare your ricotta baskets, or muslin (cheesecloth) and colander if you don't have baskets. Set them up in a baking tray so that excess liquid can drain off as it cools.

As the temperature nears 94 °C (201 °F) have a slotted spoon or fine mesh spider ready to remove the curds once they split from the whey. When the temperature reaches 94 °C (201 °F) turn off the heat and pour the vinegar into the milk while stirring in a circular motion.

Let the curds separate completely for 1–2 minutes. Remove the curds from the whey and place into your pre-prepared baskets. Cool slightly on the kitchen bench before storing in an airtight container in the fridge. Fresh ricotta will last for up to five days in the fridge, if stored properly.

The liquid remaining is called whey, and when the milk solids have separated it should be a clear yellow colour. If the whey is milky and cloudy repeat the whole process and make sure you remove all the milk solids.

RICOTTA GNOCCHI

SERVES 4 AS A SIDE DISH

Making gnocchi can be a messy process at the best of times, however Vikram, who is a dear friend of mine and a great mentor to me, taught me to pipe my gnocchi from a piping (icing) bag. I set my piping bag up with a 17 mm (½ in) nozzle and pipe even logs onto a semolina-dusted surface. Then I simply portion with a pastry card and transfer to a tray dusted with semolina until I am ready to cook them.

2 egg yolks
250 g (9 oz) ricotta, if you are using ricotta in brine hang it overnight before making the gnocchi
½ teaspoon freshly ground white pepper
2 teaspoon table salt
45 g (1½ oz/⅓ cup) plain (all-purpose) flour
125 g (4½ oz/1 cup) semolina, for dusting
extra plain (all-purpose) flour for dough

In large mixing bowl, using a spatula, combine the egg yolks and ricotta thoroughly before adding the spices and seasoning. Mix the seasoning thoroughly. When you add the flour be careful not to overwork the mix or the gnocchi will become gluey and heavy. Sift the flour into the mix a third at a time and gently combine each time. The mix will be a little sticky, however if you think that it is too wet add 1 tablespoon of flour at a time until it is a soft dough. Transfer the gnocchi to a piping (icing) bag.

Dust a working surface with semolina and pipe the gnocchi into even logs about 30 cm long, leaving 10 cm between each log. Once the gnocchi has been piped, generously dust the tops with semolina and gently roll each log to ensure they are even. Cut the logs into gnocchi. I like to cut my gnocchi as long as they are wide, however this is just my preference. Using clean dry hands transfer the gnocchi to a tray lined with baking paper and dusted in semolina.

To cook the gnocchi, boil a large pot of salted water, gently put the gnocchi into the boiling water and cook for 2½ minutes. Gently remove with a slotted spoon and serve immediately.

GRILLED FIGS WITH THYME AND RICOTTA

SERVES 6–8

2 tablespoons honey
2 teaspoons fresh thyme leaves,
    finely chopped
1 teaspoon dried lavender flowers,
    finely chopped
9 fresh black figs, cut in half
1 tablespoon extra virgin olive oil
150 g (5½ oz) fresh ricotta
100 g (3½ oz) prosciutto, thinly
    sliced
50 g (1¾ oz/⅓ cup) toasted
    walnuts, crushed
1 teaspoon freshly ground white
    pepper

Preheat your grill on high and line a baking tray with aluminium foil.

Heat the honey in a small pot on the stove over high heat, cook for 5–6 minutes or until the honey starts to caramelise and turn a deep golden colour. Add the thyme and lavender. Remove from the heat and let steep for 15 minutes.

Dress the figs in olive oil and place on the lined baking tray, cut-side down. Place the tray under the hot grill and cook for 8–10 minutes, or until the skin starts to blacken and blister. Remove the tray from under the grill and allow the figs to cool slightly.

Randomly place the figs on a serving platter, spoon over chunks of ricotta and drape the prosciutto over the top. Sprinkle the entire dish with the walnuts and white pepper. Lastly, drizzle with the honey mixture and serve.

MOZZARELLA WITH ASPARAGUS AND PEAS

SERVES 6

This is a dish that I make a lot in late spring/early summer because that is when the ingredients are at their best — the stock are on great feed and producing lots of milk around spring calving, and beans, peas and asparagus are coming into their absolute best.

200 g (7 oz) green asparagus, raw, thinly shaved

2 tablespoons lemon vinaigrette (see page 20)

pinch of sea salt

80 g (2¾ oz) fresh peas, blanched until tender

150 g (5½ oz) broad beans, shelled and blanched until tender

1 tablespoon extra virgin olive oil

400 g (14 oz) fresh mozzarella

PEA PUREE

100 g (3½ oz) frozen peas

20 g (¾ oz) unsalted butter

1 tablespoon cream

pinch of table salt

squeeze of fresh lemon juice

TO SERVE

½ cup fresh basil leaves

40 g (1½ oz/¼ cup) blanched almonds, roasted and chopped

½ teaspoon freshly ground black pepper

extra lemon vinaigrette

Make the pea puree by boiling the frozen peas in a pot of salted water. Strain the water and discard. Place peas into a food processor and with the motor running add the butter, cream, salt and lemon juice. Blitz on high for 2–3 minutes, occasionally scraping the sides of the bowl with a spatula. Check seasoning when you have finished and pass the mixture through a fine sieve, into a bowl ready to assemble the salad. This will remove the tough skin.

Dress the shaved asparagus with the lemon vinaigrette and a pinch of salt, and set aside while you assemble the salad.

Dress the fresh peas and broad beans with the olive oil and a pinch of salt in a small mixing bowl.

Now that everything is dressed you can assemble the salad. Spoon pea puree randomly over the platter, tear the mozzarella over the pea puree, spoon the broad beans and peas over the puree, scatter the entire dish with shaved asparagus and, finally, tear the basil leaves and sprinkle with chopped almonds. A final drizzle of lemon vinaigrette and cracked black pepper, and serve.

KANGAROO PIES

MAKES 6

I love cooking with kangaroo; it's a very good source of lean protein and I quite often substitute kangaroo into my red meat recipes. I use Paroo kangaroo products for the consistency and quality. If you aren't completely sold on kangaroo yet, this recipe will work great with lamb or beef. Another hint I will offer: if you want to speed up the process don't be afraid to use store bought (good quality) puff pastry.

500 g (1 lb 2 oz) kangaroo fillet
1½ tablespoons vegetable oil
¾ teaspoon table salt
1 brown onion, finely diced
2 fresh tomatoes, finely diced
100 g (3½ oz) button mushrooms,
    roughly chopped
2 garlic cloves, finely chopped
1½ teaspoons coriander powder
1 teaspoon cumin powder
½ teaspoon cinnamon powder
1 star anise
150 ml (5 fl oz/⅔ cup) red wine
500 ml (17 fl oz/2 cups) veal stock
1 tablespoon red wine vinegar
1 tablespoon brown sugar

TO ASSEMBLE

3 sheets puff pastry
2 egg yolks, beaten

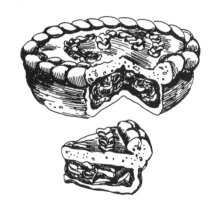

Preheat oven to 160 °C (320 °F).

Heat a large casserole pot on the stove over high heat. Add the oil and heat until just before smoking point. Season the kangaroo with salt, add it to the pot and caramelise all sides until it is a very deep brown but not burnt, 7–8 minutes. Remove the kangaroo and set aside on a plate. Add the finely diced onion and caramelise to a deep brown, 7–8 minutes. Add the tomato, mushrooms, garlic and spices and cook for a further 3–4 minutes, stirring constantly.

When the spices are aromatic and the liquid has started to reduce, deglaze the pot with the wine and reduce by half. Add the stock, vinegar and sugar, and bring to boil before placing the lid on. Turn oven up to 200 °C (400 °F) and cook in the oven for 2½ hours, or until the kangaroo is meltingly tender.

When the kangaroo is tender enough to shred, remove it from the oven and place back on the stove over medium-high heat. Reduce the liquid by half, 10–15 minutes. Allow to cool. Remove the star anise and shred the meat. The filling is now ready to make the pies.

Line six 8.5 cm (3¼ in) pie tins with the puff pastry, brushing the edges with egg wash. Divide the kangaroo filling evenly between the pie cases. Cut six rounds of puff pastry for the lids and place on top of each pie, sealing the edges using a fork. Cut three diagonal slits into the top of the lids and brush with egg wash. Bake for 20–25 minutes, or until pastry is golden brown.

KANGAROO BRESAOLA

MAKES 230–270 G

This recipe is recommended for intermediate to experienced cooks. With cured meats there are some dangers associated with the curing process and if you haven't done it before or don't know what to look for, it can make you sick. When drying bresaola, a white mould forms. This is fine and can be washed off at the end of the process with vinegar. However, a black mould can occur if the process has gone wrong and can be dangerous if you can't spot the difference. Nevertheless, it is a fun experience to cure your own meats and if you need a helping hand, make friends with your butcher and get some pointers.

500 g (1 lb 2 oz) kangaroo loin, trimmed
2 sheets muslin (cheesecloth), for the drying

CURE
40 g (1½ oz/2½ tablespoons) curing salt (see page 9)
3 teaspoons brown sugar
5 juniper berries, crushed
2 bay leaves
2 teaspoons mountain pepper, crushed
3 sprigs thyme

In a large zip-lock bag combine the curing mix with the kangaroo loin, making sure you completely cover the fillets with the cure mix. Seal the bag, squeezing as much air out of it as you can before putting it into your fridge for ten days. Every second day flip the bag to ensure even curing.

After ten days of curing, remove the loin and rinse in ice water briefly to remove excess salt. Dry the loin thoroughly with paper towel and wrap in muslin (cheesecloth). At this point, weigh the loin on a set of scales: you'll need this measurement to compare to after it has dried.

To dry the loin, lay it onto a wire rack on a baking tray and place the tray into the bottom of your fridge.

After two weeks weigh your kangaroo loin, depending on your fridge the drying time may vary. Once the loin has lost 35–40 per cent of its total weight—that's why you weighed the fillets at the start of the process—remove the loin from the fridge and unwrap it. Rinse any white mould off with white vinegar and dry again with paper towel. Rub some olive oil over the surface and keep wrapped in a clean tea towel while in the fridge. Use within two weeks of finishing the curing process.

Serve with pickled onions, cornichons and crusty bread.

TOP END BUFFALO

Geoff and Sharon Arthurs

Buffalo milk and the products that come from it are no longer an obscurity in Australia, with both chefs and home cooks using it more and more (and not just buffalo mozzarella on the ol' faithful Margherita pizza). While mozzarella is arguably the most commonly sought after product from buffalo milk, there is an ever growing list of products being produced by the innovative buffalo dairy industry. To keep up with the growing demand for

buffalo milk and to ensure quality, buffalo farmers are constantly seeking out bloodlines lines of the Riverine Buffalo from overseas.

Among this growing industry are Geoff and Sharon Arthurs, based in the iconic bush of the Top End, just over an hour's drive from Darwin.

This unusual location gives them the title of the only buffalo dairy in a semi-arid

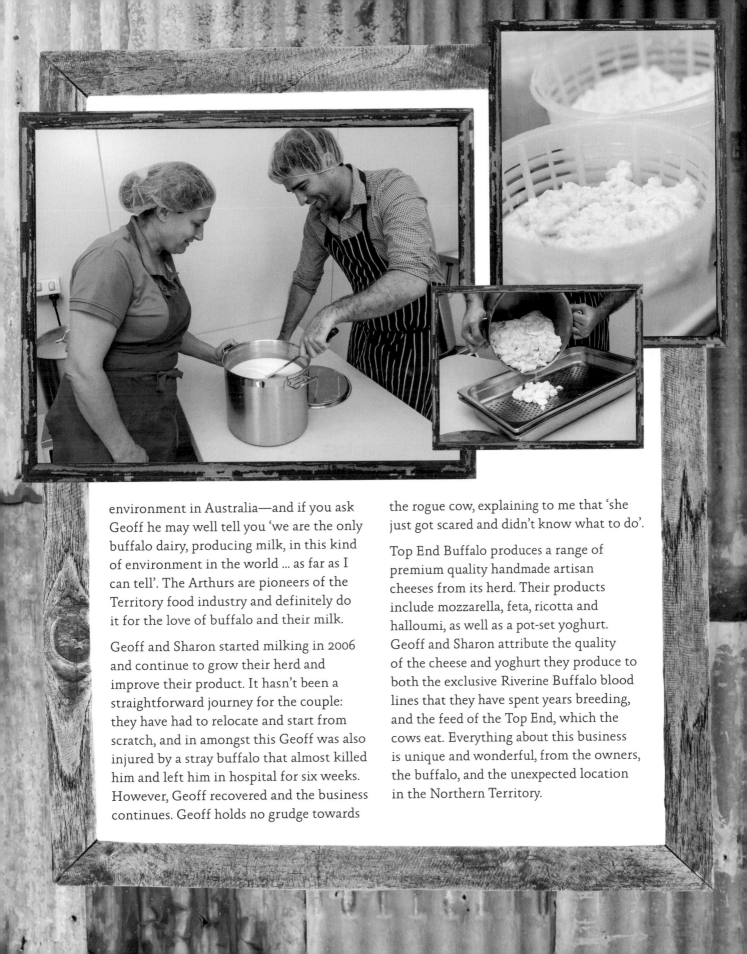

environment in Australia—and if you ask Geoff he may well tell you 'we are the only buffalo dairy, producing milk, in this kind of environment in the world ... as far as I can tell'. The Arthurs are pioneers of the Territory food industry and definitely do it for the love of buffalo and their milk.

Geoff and Sharon started milking in 2006 and continue to grow their herd and improve their product. It hasn't been a straightforward journey for the couple: they have had to relocate and start from scratch, and in amongst this Geoff was also injured by a stray buffalo that almost killed him and left him in hospital for six weeks. However, Geoff recovered and the business continues. Geoff holds no grudge towards the rogue cow, explaining to me that 'she just got scared and didn't know what to do'.

Top End Buffalo produces a range of premium quality handmade artisan cheeses from its herd. Their products include mozzarella, feta, ricotta and halloumi, as well as a pot-set yoghurt. Geoff and Sharon attribute the quality of the cheese and yoghurt they produce to both the exclusive Riverine Buffalo blood lines that they have spent years breeding, and the feed of the Top End, which the cows eat. Everything about this business is unique and wonderful, from the owners, the buffalo, and the unexpected location in the Northern Territory.

GOAT COOKED IN YOGHURT

SERVES 6

2 tablespoons vegetable oil
2 brown onions, finely sliced
1 tablespoon table salt
3 teaspoons sumac
2 teaspoons cumin
2 teaspoons coriander
1 tablespoon fresh thyme
500 g (1 lb 2 oz/2 cups)
    Greek-style yoghurt
250 ml (8½ fl oz/1 cup) chicken
    stock
1 teaspoon tumeric
1 x 2–2.5 kg (4 lb 6 oz–5½ lb)
    goat shoulder
3 tablespoons brown sugar

Preheat oven to 140 °C (275 °F).

Heat the vegetable oil in a large frying pan over high heat. Add the onions, stirring occasionally while they brown for 5–6 minutes. Add all the spices except the turmeric and cook for a further 1–2 minutes, stirring constantly. Add the yoghurt, stock and turmeric and bring to boil. Place the goat shoulder on a large piece of aluminium foil in a deep baking tray. Pour the mixture over the goat shoulder, tightly wrap it in the aluminium foil and cook in the oven for 4½ hours.

In the final hour of cooking remove the aluminium foil and increase the temperature of your oven to 180 °C (400 °F), to brown the goat before serving.

Remove the goat from the oven, and skim off as much fat from the cooking liquid as possible. Remove the goat from the liquid and wrap it in another piece of aluminium foil. Allow it to rest on a serving platter while you prepare the sauce.

Transfer the cooking liquid to a food processor. Add the brown sugar and process on high for 3–4 minutes. Pass it through a fine sieve and pour over the goat.

MAGPIE GOOSE WITH CHERRIES

SERVES 4

Magpie goose meat is seasonal, dictated by the hunting period through September. Good quality meat is available throughout this time, however for the rest of the year it is frozen. If you can't find good quality magpie goose meat, duck is a good substitute in this dish.

4 magpie goose breasts, skin scored (or the same amount of duck breasts)
1¼ teaspoons table salt
1 tablespoon olive oil
4 cups organic spinach, washed
squeeze of lemon juice

CHERRY SAUCE

100 g (3½ oz) pitted cherries
80 ml (2½ fl oz/⅓ cup) port
¼ teaspoon mountain pepper, if you cannot find mountain pepper, black pepper will suffice
½ stick cinnamon
60 ml (2 fl oz/¼ cup) brown sauce (see page 25)
20 g (¾ oz) unsalted butter

Preheat a large heavy-based pan over medium–high heat. Season the magpie goose breasts evenly with 1 teaspoon of salt on the skin side. Cook the magpie goose skin-side down for 7–8 minutes, until golden brown. Flip the breasts and cook for a further 4–5 minutes on the flesh side. Remove the breasts and let rest for 8–10 minutes in a warm spot.

Meanwhile, make the cherry sauce. In a small saucepan combine the cherries, port, pepper and cinnamon, and bring to boil. Reduce the port by two-thirds. Add the brown sauce and remove from the heat. Stir the butter through and set aside.

Heat the olive oil in a frying pan over high heat. Add the spinach and sauté for 2–3 minutes, or until just cooked but not slimy. Season with the lemon juice and pinch of salt.

To serve, slice the breasts crossways into five or six pieces. Divide the spinach evenly between four plates, place the magpie goose on top of the spinach and spoon the cherry sauce over it all.

CAMEL BRAISED IN DATE AND CINNAMON

SERVES 4–6

I really enjoy eating camel and this dish is a favourite of mine. If you are not big on the 'gamey' flavour of different types of meat, camel is a good starting point because the taste is very similar to beef. Cooking camel shoulder with a simple mix of spices and sweet dates turns this generally tough and underused cut of meat into a mouth-watering dish. This dish is a one-pot wonder.

2 tablespoons olive oil
1 kg (2 lb 3 oz) camel shoulder, cut into 3 cm (1¼ in) chunks (or beef as an alternative)
healthy pinch of table salt
1 onion, diced
3 garlic cloves, roughly chopped
1½ teaspoons ground cumin
1½ teaspoons ground coriander
1 teaspoon paprika
1 teaspoon freshly ground pepper
pinch of saffron thread
1 litre (34 fl oz/4 cups) chicken stock
400 g (14 oz) diced tomatoes
120 g (4½ oz/¾ cup) pitted dates, halved

Preheat the oven to 140 °C (275 °F).

Start by heating a large casserole pot on your stovetop. When it is hot, drizzle in the oil, season the camel meat with salt and brown the pieces. Be careful not to do too much at once as the meat will stew rather than brown—to avoid this, brown the meat in two or three batches. Once the last of the camel has been cooked and removed from the pot, caramelise the onion and garlic for 4–5 minutes. Then add the spices and cook for a further minute or two. Return the camel to the pot and deglaze with chicken stock. Add the tomatoes and dates and bring to boil.

It's time to put the lid on and get the casserole pot into the oven. Cook for 3 hours, or until the camel is meltingly tender. If you feel like being traditional, serve this dish with frekeh—otherwise rice is just as good.

DATE MEATBALLS WITH TOMATO AND CAPSICUM SAUCE

SERVES 4–6

MEATBALLS

750 g (1 lb 11 oz) lamb, minced (ground), not lean mince
1 teaspoon ground coriander
1½ teaspoons ground cumin
100 g (3½ oz/⅔ cup) pitted dates, chopped
75 g (2¾ oz/½ cup) pistachios, roughly chopped
1 teaspoon table salt

SAUCE

2 tomatoes, halved
1 red capsicum (bell pepper)
100 g (3½ oz) button mushrooms
1 onion, halved
2 garlic cloves
200 ml (7 fl oz/¾ cup) chicken stock
2 tablespoons sherry vinegar
1 teaspoon table salt

Preheat oven to 200 °C (400 °F).

Place your sauce ingredients into a large roasting tray and pop into the oven. Roast until all the vegetables are soft, around 45–50 minutes. A little charring of the vegetables is fine, however too much will overpower the dish. To prevent this, turn the vegetables after 25 minutes. Once the vegetables are soft—check by piercing with a fork or skewer—transfer everything to your food processor and blitz on high for 3–4 minutes. Set aside.

To make the meatballs, in a large mixing bowl combine all of the ingredients thoroughly with a wooden spoon, working the mix into the sides of the bowl. There are no eggs to bind the meatballs in this recipe so it is important to work the meatball mix vigorously for 3–4 minutes to achieve the correct texture. Once the ingredients are thoroughly mixed it is time to make the meatballs—you can wear gloves to eliminate a lot of mess but they aren't essential. I like my meatballs no bigger than a golf ball, 3–4 cm (1¼ in) across is a great size, but feel free to make them as big or as small as you like. Once all the meatballs have been formed, brown them in a large sauté pan, being mindful that because of the dates the meatballs can burn easily, so don't leave them alone for too long.

Once the meatballs have all been browned pour the vegetable sauce over them and simmer for 15–20 minutes. I love to serve this over warm cheesy polenta, however, there are no rules so feel free to mix it up.

SMOKED BUFFALO TARTAR

SERVES 8–10

Whenever I get my hands on good quality fresh buffalo I generally make a raw dish because it's a beautiful delicious, deep red, meat. (If buffalo is cooked incorrectly it dries out very quickly, becoming tough and rubbery.) Smoking it at home is fun and a great way to try to use different flavours. I use all sorts of smoking chips, teas and dried herbs. To make this recipe very simple you will need a steamer insert, a lid that fits the steamer and a pot that the steamer fits into snugly. I don't support it, but if you want to be a cowboy there is such a thing as liquid smoke, which you can add to the tartar when you add the rest of the ingredients.

400 g (14 oz) buffalo eye fillet
a large handful of fine, hickory
    smoking chips
1 tablespoon tea, your favourite
    style
1 tablespoon cornichons, chopped
1 tablespoon capers, chopped
1 tablespoon banana shallot, finely
    diced
3 teaspoons dijon mustard
½ tablespoon extra virgin olive oil
½ tablespoon worcestershire sauce
5 squirts tobasco
3 teaspoons fresh lemon juice
3 teaspoons sea salt

TO SERVE
shaved parmesan
toasted sourdough

To start you will have to smoke the buffalo fillet. Place the fillet on a small side plate and into the steamer insert with a few cubes of ice. Tear off a piece of baking paper that is larger than the steamer and place that over the top, seal the steamer with the lid and have ready the pot that the steamer fits into. You may want to line the pot with aluminium foil if you are worried about staining the bottom of it from the smoking chips.

In a large stainless steel pan (or old pan that's due for the bin), heat the smoking chips and tea over the hottest burner on your stovetop. This will take 5–10 minutes to really start to smoke—if the chips catch on fire that's fine, just smother the flame with a pan the same size. When the chips are completely black and smoking fiercely, tip the chips into the pot and place the covered steamer over the top, drape a tea towel over the entire set up and leave for 10 minutes. The buffalo fillet is now ready. If you prefer a smokier flavour repeat the above process after chilling your meat in the fridge. Smoking the meat can be done in advance. It will last two to three days in your fridge once smoked.

To make the tartar, dice the buffalo fillet into 3–4 mm (¼ in) chunks and place it into a large mixing bowl. Add all the seasoning ingredients and combine well with a fork. Check for taste.

Serve the tartar on toasted sourdough with freshly shaved parmesan.

ROPER RIVER BRAHMANS
Daniel and Shannon Tapp

Three hours' drive from the nearest town, down a single-lane road with the last 50 kilometres (31 miles) on dirt doesn't sound appealing to a lot of people, however, for Daniel and Shannon Tapp it's home. Daniel and Shannon are both third-generation cattle producers and have lived on cattle stations all their lives. They own over 68,796 hectares (170,000 acres) that run 5000 head of Brahmans in the heart of the Roper River Region of the Top End. They have worked tirelessly for the past seventeen years building the property from the ground up. Daniel explained to me that when they first moved there, there was nothing but a couple of old boundary fences and a few broken troughs. The first few years were tough, living out of swags and only running the generator through the night so they could have electricity to

cool the fridge and run the fans so they could sleep.

For the Tapps, even in the early days, dinnertime was always important, 'It was a time of the day we could just relax and enjoy where we lived and what we were doing.' Whether at the beginning with just Daniel and Shannon cooking sparse meals over a fire, or right up to present day with two young daughters and everyone helping in the kitchen, the family meal has been an important part of their daily station life.

Living in such a remote region of Australia means that a trip to the grocery store is not a daily occurrence … not even a fortnightly occurrence. In fact, Daniel,

Shannon and their daughters take a trip to Katherine to obtain supplies once a month. Not being able to get to town much, coupled with a constant supply of meat, means the basis of a lot of their meals is beef, which is broken up with a few vegetables. The terminology 'meat and three veg' definitely applies to the food served on the Tapp's property.

Despite the adversity faced by the Tapps living in such a remote region, Daniel has never considered farming beef anywhere else. He believes the chemical-free, natural pastures of the Northern Territory give his cattle a superior quality, making it an overall healthier product for human consumption.

8-HOUR SLOW-COOKED LAMB SHOULDER WITH ANCHOVY BUTTER

SERVES 6

2–2.5 kg (4 lb 6 oz–5½ lb) lamb
  shoulder
2 teaspoons table salt

ANCHOVY BUTTER

100 g (3½ oz) unsalted butter,
  softened
grated zest of 2 lemons
50 g (1¾ oz) anchovy fillets
1 tablespoon dijon mustard
1 tablespoon fresh thyme leaves
2 teaspoons table salt

Preheat oven to 120 °C (248 °F).

In a food processor blitz all the ingredients for the anchovy butter on high for 2–3 minutes, until everything is incorporated. Scrape the butter from the food processor and transfer to a bowl for use throughout the cooking of the lamb.

Place the lamb shoulder onto a roasting tray and season with the salt. Rub half of the anchovy butter over the lamb shoulder and cover the roasting tray tightly with aluminium foil. Put it into the oven. Cook for 8 hours.

In the final hour of cooking remove the aluminium foil and increase the temperature of the oven to 200 °C (400 °F) . Baste the shoulder with half of the remaining compound butter and cook uncovered for 40–45 minutes.

Remove the lamb from the oven. Cover in aluminium foil and allow to rest for 20 minutes. Just as you serve the lamb brush on the last of the anchovy butter.

PAN-FRIED LAMB SWEETBREADS

SERVES 4

Sweetbreads need prepping before you can use them in the final dish, but don't let this deter you because this ingredient is absolutely worth the effort and can be used in a wide array of dishes. Start this recipe a few hours before you need the sweetbreads. Place your raw sweetbreads into a plastic container and cover in cold water and let soak for 2–3 hours in the fridge. The sweetbreads do benefit if this process is repeated once. Drain the sweetbreads and rinse, place into a pot and completely cover the sweetbreads in cold water, season with a pinch of salt and a squeeze of lemon juice. Bring to boil over high heat, and boil for 4–5 minutes before straining the sweetbreads and submerging them in ice water. Once the sweetbreads are ice cold, dry them on paper towel and, with a small sharp knife, trim any veins, sinew and dark spots, and peel the outer membrane off with your fingers. If you have big sweetbreads cut them on a bias into 15 mm thick medallions. Store on paper towel until ready to cook.

2 tablespoons olive oil
500 g (1 lb 2 oz) lamb
    sweetbreads, prepared as above
1 teaspoon table salt
150 g (5½ oz/1 cup) semolina

SAUCE

60 ml (2 fl oz/¼ cup) white wine
60 g (2 oz) unsalted butter, cubed
½ cup flat-leaf parsley, finely
    chopped
1 tablespoon shallot, finely minced
1 tablespoons capers, finely
    chopped
¼ teaspoon table salt
2 tablespoons fresh lemon juice
¼ teaspoon freshly ground white
    pepper

In a small saucepan. Over medium heat, reduce the white wine by half. Add the butter a quarter at a time, whisking in completely before adding the next bit of butter. After the butter has been completely melted into the reduced white wine add the parsley, shallot and capers, and warm through for 2–3 minutes. Remove the pot from the heat and season with salt, lemon juice and freshly ground white pepper. Keep warm until sweetbreads are cooked.

Heat the olive oil in a large frying pan over medium–high heat. In a deep tray season the sweetbreads firstly with the salt before dusting them with the semolina. Cook the sweetbreads for 4–6 minutes, or until cooked through, turning once. Rest the sweetbreads on paper towel for 2–3 minutes to absorb excess oil. Serve with the parsley and caper sauce generously spooned over the top.

LAMB RACKS WITH PRUNE JAM

SERVES 6–8

2 × 8 point lamb racks, trimmed
1½ teaspoons table salt
150 g (5½ oz/½ cup) whole
    prunes, or 3 prunes each
1½ teaspoons earl grey tea leaves
2 tablespoons honey

TO SERVE

20–25 chicory (endive) leaves
80 ml (2½ fl oz/⅓ cup) brown
    sauce (see page 25)

Preheat oven to 200 °C (400 °F).

Heat a large ovenproof pan over medium–high heat. Season the lamb racks with the salt and place fat-side down into the hot pan. Cook the racks for 8–10 minutes, until the fat starts to render and is golden brown. Flip the lamb racks so that the fat side is up and place the pan with the racks into the hot oven. Cook for 15–20 minutes, or until cooked to your liking. If you have a meat probe, I like to serve my lamb between 56–58 °C (132–136 °F) internal temperature at the thickest part, generally the middle. Rest the lamb for 10 minutes in aluminium foil after removing from the oven.

Meanwhile, make the prune jam. In a small saucepan add the prunes, earl grey tea leaves and enough water to cover the prunes. Bring to a rapid boil and cook uncovered for 10 minutes.

As the prunes boil, caramelise the honey. Place the honey in a small saucepan over medium–high heat and cook for 6–8 minutes, until the honey has become deep brown in colour and is very aromatic.

When three-quarters of the liquid has evaporated from the prunes add them to the caramalised honey and toss to combine. Set aside and keep warm.

Portion the lamb racks, two to three points per person, and serve with the prunes in honey, brown sauce and fresh chicory (endive) leaves.

GRILLED LAMB FILLET WITH WHITE ONION PUREE

SERVES 4

4 × 200 g (7 oz) lamb fillets
1 tablespoon table salt
1½ tablespoons vegetable oil

ONION PUREE

1 tablespoon vegetable oil
3 medium white onions, very finely
    sliced
250 ml (8½ fl oz/1 cup) water
½ teaspoon table salt
3 tablespoon cream
20 g (¾ oz) unsalted butter

TO SERVE

80 ml (2½ fl oz/⅓ cup) brown
    sauce (see page 25)
1 cup watercress
freshly ground black pepper

Heat 1 tablespoon of the vegetable oil in a heavy saucepan over medium–high heat. Add the onion and cook until translucent, stirring constantly for 10–12 minutes. Do not brown the onions. Add the cup of water, reduce the heat to a simmer, cover and cook for 20 minutes, or until onions are completely soft. Stir the onions occasionally, keeping an eye on them to ensure they don't colour. Remove the lid and cook off most of the liquid while stirring constantly, for 8–10 minutes. Once again do not colour the onions as this will taint the colour of your puree. Transfer the onions to a food processor, add the salt, cream and butter, and blitz on high for 4–5 minutes. Pass the puree through a sieve and check the seasoning. Keep warm until the lamb is ready.

Heat a large chargrill pan over high heat. Season the lamb fillets with the salt and oil. Cook the lamb for 6–8 minutes, or until they are cooked to your liking. Rest in a warm place for 5–10 minutes.

Serve each fillet with the onion puree, using the brown sauce, fresh watercress and black pepper to garnish.

BEEF RIBS WITH MASHED POTATO AND LENTILS

SERVES 4

I love to braise and slow cook my meat. If you want to use another cut for this recipe, beef cheek would also work exceptionally well. I make a creamy mash potato with a tamis, however you can use a good old potato masher.

RIBS

4 × 350 g (12½ oz) beef ribs
1 teaspoon table salt
1 tablespoon vegetable oil
1 brown onion, peeled and cut into
   6–8 wedges
1 carrot, roughly sliced
4 sprigs thyme
1 sprig rosemary
8 black peppercorns
500 ml (17 fl oz/2 cups) beef stock

MASHED POTATO

500 g (1 lb 2 oz) royal blue potato,
   any mashing variety will do
630 g (1 lb 6 oz/2 cups) rock salt,
   for baking
70 ml (2¼ fl oz/¼ cup) cream
70 ml (2¼ fl oz/¼ cup) milk
50 g (1¾ oz) unsalted butter
2 teaspoons table salt
pinch of freshly ground white pepper

LENTIL SAUCE

2 teaspoons olive oil
½ brown onion, finely diced
1 stick celery, finely diced
100 g (3½ oz) green lentils, soaked
250 ml (8½ fl oz/1 cup) chicken stock
½ cup brown sauce (see page 25)

Preheat oven to 160 °C (320 °F).

Season the beef ribs with salt and brown them with the vegetable oil in a heavy casserole pot (that has a lid) over high heat for 8–10 minutes. Add the onion, carrot and herbs and spices, sauté for 2–3 minutes. Add the stock, cover with the lid and bake for 3½ hours, or until meltingly tender. For the final hour of the cooking time remove the lid.

Roast the potatoes with the rock salt in a shallow roasting tray uncovered for 1 hour, or until completely soft. The rock salt isn't essential, however it does draw out moisture which will then concentrate the flavour of your mashed potato. Allow potatoes to cool slightly before peeling.

Gently heat the cream, milk, butter and seasoning in a small pot and keep warm. With a pastry card or spatula, push the peeled potatoes through the tamis into a medium-sized saucepan—doing a small amount at a time will make the process quicker. While the potatoes are still warm, slowly incorporate the warm cream–butter mixture using a spatula. Check for seasoning. Mashed potato can hold for hours, just cover with plastic wrap so it does not dry, and gently warm it with a little cream when you want to use it.

In a medium saucepan heat the oil and caramelise the onion and celery for 5–6 minutes. Add the lentils and sauté for 2–3 minutes. Add the stock. Bring to boil over high heat, reduce to a simmer and cook for 25–30 minutes, or until the lentils are tender but not soft. Remove from the stove and add the brown sauce. Mix thoroughly.

Serve the ribs with the creamy mash and lentil sauce.

GAME BUTCHER

Patrick Carmody

Patrick Carmody has made his life out of game meat. He calls himself the conservational butcher.

Patrick moved to the Territory in 1963 as a young boy with his family, for the opening of the Katherine meatworks, Northern Meat Exports. Shortly after moving up he started his own business, supplying game meat to the pet meat industry. This led to a career in land conservation as a wildlife ranger, eradicating feral animals for the Northern Territory Government. As an animal welfare advocate he rose to the top of the Wildlife Rangers in the feral animal eradication program. He believes that the introduced species are now here to stay and it is up to us to manage them humanely and sustainably for the benefit of the native flora and fauna. It is in this role that Patrick saw a gap in the market

where feral animals were being killed to control their population yet not utilised for the benefit of the local community. Patrick knows first-hand the importance of not wasting any of the animal, no matter what it may be. He says that in Australia we have never had to eat anything but beef and lamb, which is a shame because a lot of the game meat we have is very healthy and tastes great, and there is no reason why it shouldn't be a more common choice when it comes to choosing your next meal.

Patrick owns and operates a butcher shop called Jones Meat Mart, which specialises in game meat. In Jones Meat Mart you'll find everything from crocodile steaks to camel sausages. However, Patrick's favourite would be his famous buffalo burgers. I tried getting him to donate his recipe but this is a sacred recipe that he just couldn't give up ... yet.

DRY ROASTED BRISKET WITH BURNT GHERKINS

SERVES 6–8

1 × 2–2.5 kg (4 lb 6 oz–5½ lb) brisket, deckle end (the thickest end)
250 ml (8½ fl oz/1 cup) chicken stock
8 whole gherkins (pickles)
3 teaspoons extra virgin olive oil
squeeze of lemon juice

DRY RUB

1 tablespoon cumin seeds
3 teaspoons coriander seeds
2 teaspoons celery seeds
2 tablespoons table salt
1 tablespoon fennel seeds
2 teaspoons chilli flakes
2 teaspoons smoked paprika
2 teaspoons sweet paprika
2 tablespoons brown sugar
1 tablespoon dijon mustard

COLESLAW

125 ml (4 fl oz/½ cup) aioli (see page 20)
125 ml (4 fl oz/½ cup) Craig's BBQ sauce (see page 10)
¼ purple cabbage, thinly sliced
2 teaspoons sea salt
2 tablespoons lemon juice

Preheat oven to 160 °C (320 °F).

Combine all ingredients for the dry rub, except the brown sugar and dijon mustard, in a spice grinder and grind until a fine powder consistency is reached. Transfer to a small mixing bowl and mix through the dijon and brown sugar.

Completely cover the brisket in the rub and place into a roasting tray. Pour stock into the bottom of the tray and cover tightly with aluminium foil. Roast the brisket for 2½ hours before removing the foil and roasting for a further 1½ hours uncovered.

Remove the brisket from the oven and let rest while you prepare the gherkins (pickles) and coleslaw.

Using either a blowtorch or the open flame of your stovetop completely blacken the gherkins. Once the gherkins are blackened, put them in a mixing bowl and season with extra virgin olive oil, sea salt and lemon juice, before cutting them in half lengthways.

In a large mixing bowl, combine all the ingredients for the coleslaw and mix thoroughly. Let sit for 15–20 minutes before serving. Toss the coleslaw again just before you serve it.

Toast some sourdough and generously season with extra virgin olive oil.

I tear off a large sheet of baking paper, lay it on the table and serve the brisket, coleslaw, gherkins and toast in the centre for fun—and no dishes to clean!

EYE FILLET WITH PEA PESTO

SERVES 4–6

800 g (1 lb 12 oz) eye fillet
1 tablespoon vegetable oil
1 teaspoon table salt

PEA PESTO

1 cup frozen peas
¼ cup parmesan cheese, freshly grated
½ cup flat-leaf parsley
½ cup coriander (cilantro) leaves
2 tablespoons pine nuts, toasted
2½ tablespoons extra virgin olive oil
½ teaspoon sea salt
¼ teaspoon freshly ground black pepper
1 tablespoon fresh lemon juice

Preheat oven to 200 °C (400 °F).

Heat an ovenproof frying pan over medium–high heat. Season the eye fillet with the oil and salt, and brown in the pan for 6–8 minutes, until completely caramelised on all sides. Place the pan with the eye fillet into the oven and cook for 18–20 minutes for medium-rare, or until cooked to your liking. Remove from the oven, wrap in aluminium foil and rest for 10 minutes before serving.

Meanwhile, bring the peas to boil in a small saucepan of salted water. Strain the water and let them steam for a minute. Put all the ingredients for the pesto into a food processor and pulse ten to twelve times, until everything is roughly chopped and incorporated—if you prefer, you can make it smoother by turning the motor on and processing until you are happy with the consistency.

Thinly slice the eye fillet and spoon the pea pesto over it to serve.

BEEF STEW WITH PEPPER DUMPLINGS

SERVES 6–8

2 tablespoons vegetable oil

1 kg (2 lb 3 oz) beef chuck, cut into 3 cm (1¼ in) cubes

1 teaspoon table salt

2 brown onions, finely diced

2 carrots, finely diced

375 ml (12½ fl oz/1½ cup) red wine, the wine you drink

1 litre (34 fl oz/4 cups) veal stock

80 ml (2½ fl oz/⅓ cup) vino cotto

3 very ripe tomatoes, cut into chunks

2 bay leaves

1 stick cinnamon

DUMPLINGS

140 g (5 oz/1 cup) self-raising flour

45 g (1½ oz) unsalted butter

½ teaspoon table salt

½ teaspoon black pepper

2 teaspoons fresh thyme leaves

⅓ cup parmesan, freshly grated

90 ml (3 fl oz/⅓ cup) milk

Preheat oven to 160 °C (320 °F).

Heat the vegetable oil in a large casserole pot with a lid over medium–high heat. Season the chuck with salt and brown in batches until heavily caramelised, 7–8 minutes per batch. When all the chuck has been browned set it aside in a heatproof bowl.

In the same casserole pot add the onion and carrot and cook for 8–10 minutes, or until heavily caramelised. Return the chuck to the pot and deglaze with the wine, and reduce by half. Be sure to loosen anything stuck to the bottom of the pot with a wooden spoon.

Add the remaining ingredients and bring to boil. Cover with the lid and place in the oven. Cook for 2½–3 hours, or until the chuck is meltingly tender.

Dumplings are very simple to make and cook quite quickly. To make the dumplings combine the flour, butter, salt, pepper, thyme and parmesan in a food processor and blitz on high for 1–2 minutes, until the mixture resembles bread crumbs. Transfer the mixture into a large mixing bowl and make a well in the centre. Add the milk and incorporate into the mixture to form a dough using a pastry card or spatula. Do not overwork this dough as it will make for tough, chewy dumplings—think of it like a scone mix.

Divide the dough into 12–15 portions and store on a tray dusted with flour in the fridge, with a clean, damp tea towel placed over the top until ready to cook.

Around 20–25 minutes before serving, remove the lid from the casserole pot, add the dumplings, distributing evenly around the pot, and cook uncovered until ready to serve.

'THE SHOWOFF' — TOMAHAWKS ON THE BARBECUE

SERVES 4–6

2 tomahawk steaks
12–15 padron peppers
4 large shallots, with skin on,
    cut in half lengthways
1½ teaspoons table salt
3 tablespoons vegetable oil

TO SERVE

2 tablespoons lemon vinaigrette
    (see page 20)
80 ml (2½ fl oz/⅓ cup) brown
    sauce (see page 25)
freshly ground black pepper

Preheat the grill on your barbecue and ensure that you have given it a good clean. Separately season the steaks, padrons and shallots with the salt and oil.

Grill the tomahawk steaks for 15–20 minutes, turning occasionally until nicely charred. Rest them in your barbecue's roasting racks for 20–25 minutes, or until the steak is cooked to your liking. If you are not confident cooking your steaks without set times I would suggest using a meat probe with this recipe as cooking time and temps will vary drastically from barbecue to barbecue. I serve my tomahawks at an internal temperature of 57 °C (134 °F).

Grill the padrons and shallots, turning occasionally until tender and charred, around 10–12 minutes. Season with lemon vinaigrette when cooked.

I slice the tomahawks after resting them and then serve them with the grilled padrons and shallots scattered around, and a healthy serve of brown sauce and freshly ground black pepper over everything.

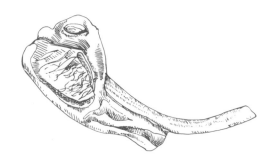

SOMETHING SWEET

SOMETHING
SWEET

Desserts and sweets always give me a sense of nostalgia and a rush of excitement, whether I am eating them or making them. They transport me back to my childhood on the stations. Having any sweet treat was a rare occasion, and generally it would be spurred on by someone from town coming out to visit us. With the impending visit approaching mum would spend hours in the tiny kitchen, in forty-degree heat, preparing either her famous self-saucing pudding or her pavlova—a hit for everyone involved.

The stations were a little behind the times, the staple lolly was a jube, the soft drink of choice was either cream soda or sarsaparilla, and there was enough corned beef and white sauce to sink a ship. Needless to say, the desserts were no different, heavily influenced by the property's European heritage. Puddings seemed to be a staple ... rice pudding, bread and butter pudding, golden syrup pudding, chocolate pudding and, if you had nothing to flavour it, obviously steamed pudding by itself. Possibly one of my favourites, though, was Sao pudding.

Accompanying most of the desserts was tinned fruit and custard, and that's powdered custard with vanilla essence and water, not the real custard made with eggs, cream and milk. I loved it—though if it is all you know then it is hard to be discerning. Obviously, perishables would not survive. Everything had to last for at least a month as this was the average time between store runs.

Another ingredient that was a staple in station life was lard. At the start of every year dad would buy two or three drums of the stuff from the stock feed store and it would be used for everything from making doughs and pastries, frying, cooking steaks, and I even remember the older workers using it to oil their boots. For the sake of everyone's arteries, and ease of making the recipes, I haven't used any lard in this chapter. I have also cut down on the puddings, reluctantly. However, I have taken a lot of the classics from my childhood and re-created them.

MILLIONAIRE MACADAMIAS

MAKES 24 SQUARES

If you make this and take it along to one of your social events it will definitely win over the masses. However, it's just as good to make and keep at home for you to indulge in. Now, don't let the use of condensed milk and milk chocolate deter you and make you think of it as an inferior product. Once you make this slice it will be in your very own arsenal of party pleasing dishes.

BASE

155 g (5½ oz/1 cup) plain (all-purpose) flour
155 g (5½ oz/1¾ cups) desiccated (shredded) coconut
50 g (1¾ oz/⅓ cup) macadamia nuts, roasted and finely chopped
1 teaspoon baking powder
145 g (5 oz/⅔ cup) caster (superfine) sugar
160 g (5½ oz) unsalted butter, softened

FILLING

150 g (5½ oz) unsalted butter
150 g (5½ oz/1 cup) brown sugar
600 ml (20½ fl oz/2½ cups) condensed milk
2½ tablespoons golden syrup
1 teaspoon vanilla extract
150 g (5½ oz/1 cup) macadamia nuts, roughly chopped, some left whole

TOPPING

400 g (14 oz) milk chocolate

Preheat oven to 180 °C (250 °F).

Place all ingredients for the base in a bowl and mix until well combined. Press mixture firmly into a 22 cm x 32 cm (8¾ in × 12½ in) baking tray lined with baking paper. Bake for 10–12 minutes. It should be lightly golden.

Place all ingredients for the caramel filling, except for the macadamia nuts, in a saucepan and stir over a low heat. Continue to stir until all the brown sugar is dissolved. Cook the caramel for a further 8–10 minutes, being careful not to let the caramel burn.

Scatter the macadamias over the cooked base before pouring the caramel filling evenly over the base. Place the tray back in the oven for 10 minutes to cook the caramel. Remove from the oven and allow to cool completely.

To finish the slice, melt the chocolate in a bowl over a saucepan of hot water. It is also really quick and easy to heat chocolate in the microwave but watch it closely because it will burn quickly. Spread the melted chocolate over the caramel, taking care to cover all sections of the slice evenly. Place the slice in the fridge to set the chocolate. Once the chocolate is hard, you can cut the slice into squares.

ANZAC BISCUITS

MAKES 20–25

ANZAC biscuits are a staple. You have to have a stock standard recipe on hand to whip up at the last minute for unexpected guests. With this recipe I use my wattle seed butter to give it a point of difference. However, you can use plain unsalted butter instead if you wish, but you should increase the amount of caster (superfine) sugar in the recipe.

120 g (4½ oz) wattle seed butter (see page 6)
2 tablespoons golden syrup
150 g (5½ oz/1 cup) plain (all-purpose) flour
100 g (3½ oz/1 cup) rolled (porridge) oats
45 g (1½ oz/½ cup) desiccated (shredded) coconut
75 g (2¾ oz/½ cup) raw macadamias, roughly chopped
115 g (4 oz/½ cup) caster (superfine) sugar
1 teaspoon bicarbonate of soda (baking soda)
1 tablespoon boiling water

Preheat the oven to 180 °C (350 °F) and line two baking trays with baking paper.

Gently melt the wattle seed butter with the golden syrup in a small saucepan over low heat.

Meanwhile, sieve the plain flour into a large mixing bowl. Mix in the oats, coconut, macadamias and sugar, and make a well in the centre.

Mix the bicarbonate of soda with the boiling water and stir it into the melted butter mixture. Pour the butter mixture into the well of the dry ingredients and thoroughly combine using a spatula.

Make tablespoon-sized balls (about the size of a large strawberry) and place them on the lined baking trays at least 2–3 cm (¾ in–1¼ in) apart. Slightly flatten the dough with your palm before placing the trays into the oven and cooking for 12–15 minutes. Cool the biscuits on cake racks before serving.

EVERY-CHOC CHOC CHIP COOKIES

MAKES 40–50

150 g (5½ oz/1 cup) plain (all-purpose) flour

150 g (5½ oz/1 cup) plain wholemeal (whole-wheat) flour

1 teaspoon baking powder

½ teaspoon sea salt

250 g (9 oz) unsalted butter

140 g (5 oz/¾ cup) brown sugar

115 g (4 oz/½ cup) caster (superfine) sugar

2 teaspoons vanilla paste

2 tablespoons maple syrup

1 egg

2 tablespoons milk

200 g (7 oz) dark chocolate, roughly chopped

200 g (7 oz) white chocolate, roughly chopped

200 g (7 oz) milk chocolate, roughly chopped

150 g (5½ oz/1 cup) hazelnuts, skin off

150 g (5½ oz/1 cup) raw macadamia nuts

Preheat oven to 180 °C (350 °F) and line two baking trays with baking paper.

Sieve flours, baking powder and salt into a bowl and set aside.

Using an electric mixer on high, cream the butter with the two types of sugars for 6–7 minutes. With the motor running mix in the vanilla paste, maple syrup, egg and milk until everything is fully combined.

Fold the flour mixture into the creamed butter with a spatula, until completely incorporated. Then stir through all the chocolate until thoroughly mixed. The dough should come away from the sides—if the dough is too sticky, sift in a little flour at a time until a soft dough comes together.

Form tablespoon-sized balls and place them 2–3 cm (¾ in–1¼ in) apart on the baking trays. Flatten the balls slightly with your palm. Place the trays into the oven and bake for 12–15 minutes, or until golden.

Allow to cool before serving.

FRESH SCONES

450 g (1 lb/3 cups) self-raising
  flour, plus extra for dusting
2 teaspoons baking powder
2 tablespoons caster (superfine)
  sugar
small pinch of sea salt
250 ml (8½ fl oz/1 cup) full-cream
  (whole) milk
250 ml (8½ fl oz/1 cup) full
  (whole) cream

EGG WASH

1 egg yolk
2 tablespoons milk

Preheat oven to 200 °C (400 °F).

Sift the dry ingredients twice into a large mixing bowl, add the milk and cream and mix together with a knife until just combined.

Turn the dough onto a floured surface and knead until the dough just comes together. Roll the dough out into a 2.5 cm (1 in) thick disc and cut out rounds with a 4 cm (1½ in) or 5 cm (2 in) cookie cutter (if you don't have a cookie cutter, the lid of an oil spray bottle will do the job).

Transfer the scones to a lined baking tray with at least 2 cm (¾ in) between each one. Brush the tops with the egg wash and cook for 15–20 minutes.

TRACI'S PAV

SERVES 6

6 egg whites, at room temperature

230 g (8 oz/1 cup) caster
(superfine) sugar

2 teaspoons cornflour

1 teaspoon white vinegar

80 g (2¾ oz) white chocolate,
finely chopped

50 g (1¾ oz/½ cup) hazelnuts,
toasted and finely chopped

2 teaspoons cocoa

SAUCE

200 g (7 oz) fresh blueberries,
100 g (3½ oz) cut in half

1 tablespoon caster (superfine)
sugar

2 teaspoons fresh lemon juice

1½ tablespoons vodka (optional)

250 ml (8½ fl oz/1 cup) full
(whole) cream, whipped,
to serve

Preheat the oven to 160 °C (320 °F) and line a baking tray with baking paper.

Using an electric mixer, in a large mixing bowl beat the egg whites until they form soft peaks. Start to add the caster (superfine) sugar, a tablespoon at a time, until the meringue is stiff and shiny. If you rub the meringue between your fingers at this stage you shouldn't be able to feel the sugar.

With a metal spoon gently fold in the remaining ingredients until the cocoa is thoroughly mixed in. Spoon the mixture onto the prepared baking tray forming a thick, 20–25 cm circle. Place in the oven then immediately reduce the temperature to 120 °C (250 °F). Cook for 1¼ hours. Turn the oven off and leave the oven door ajar, allowing the meringue to cool completely in the oven.

Meanwhile, make the blueberry sauce. In a food processor blitz 100 g of the whole blueberries on high for 2–3 minutes, until smooth. Pass the blueberry puree through a fine sieve into a small saucepan over medium heat, discard the solids. Add the sugar and lemon juice, and gently warm to a simmer until the sugar has dissolved. Check seasoning. While still on the heat, if using, add the vodka and cook off for a further minute. Remove from heat and add the fresh blueberries. Cool in the fridge before serving.

Serve the pavlova with whipped cream and blueberry sauce.

FROM HUMBLE BEGINNINGS ...

Traci McHours (Mum)

Mum has been an integral part of my food journey and I can thank her for my initial love of cooking. Over the years we have spent countless hours in the kitchen together and on the phone discussing the latest recipes we have tried. Even as I continue to work in kitchens I still always value her advice.

Mum wasn't always a great home cook. In fact, she admits that she couldn't even boil water when she first had to cook. Mum's

first time cooking was a 'sink or swim' scenario, and according to Dad she did sink for a bit. Mum moved from the city as a young girl of seventeen to be with my (future) dad on one of the biggest cattle stations in the Northern Territory. It had plenty of mouths to feed. The only job available to her at that time was the station cook—the previous one had walked off the job. Her first dish was a stew. Mum had never cooked a stew

before, but she had seen it done plenty of times. In a big pot she combined all the essentials: potatoes, carrots, onions, pumpkins, beef, Keen's curry powder and water. It was only 9 am and, with a full day ahead of her, she turned the gas to high and left it to boil while she headed off to do some work with Dad. On returning at dinnertime she was confronted by a wall of smoke in the kitchen. There were lumps of black coal where the ingredients had

boiled dry. Her first night on the job the whole station only had bread for dinner.

Since then Mum has taught herself to be an amazing home cook. I know everyone says their mum is the best cook, well mine is. My mum has been my biggest support and has played a monumental role in my new life in food. I owe a lot of what I am doing to her.

BREAD AND BUTTER PUDDING

SERVES 6

5 egg yolks

115 g (4 oz/½ cup) caster
(superfine) sugar

300 ml (10 fl oz/1¼ cups) full
(whole) cream

200 ml (7 fl oz/¾ cup) full-cream
(whole) milk

seeds of 2 vanilla beans

400 g (14 oz) brioche loaf, cut into
2–3 cm (¾ in–1¼ in) slices

200 g (7 oz) fresh pitted cherries,
canned pitted black cherries,
drained can be substituted

50 g (1¾ oz) currants, rehydrated
in hot water for 20 minutes
and drained

2½ tablespoons brandy

CHOCOLATE SAUCE

250 ml (8½ fl oz/1 cup) full
(whole) cream

100 g (3½ oz) dark chocolate

20 g (¾ oz) unsalted butter

Preheat oven to 180 °C (350 °F) and grease a 1.5–1.75 litre (51 fl oz–60 fl oz/6–7 cup) capacity ovenproof dish.

In a large mixing bowl combine the egg yolks and sugar, and whisk until pale and creamy. Add cream, milk and vanilla seeds, and mix well.

Cut the brioche slices diagonally in half and stand them up in the ovenproof dish. Scatter the cherries and the currants around in the dish, getting them in between the slices also. Pour the cream mixture and brandy over the brioche, and cover in plastic wrap. Let steep for 10 minutes so the brioche can absorb the flavours. This can be done hours in advance, just sit it in the fridge until you are ready to bake.

Bake in the oven for 25–30 minutes, until the bread is golden and the liquid has almost totally been absorbed.

Meanwhile, make the chocolate sauce. Heat the cream over a low heat until just before boiling point. Do not boil. Blitz the dark chocolate in a food processor until it's a fine powder and, with the motor running, slowly pour in the hot cream. Add the butter and process for a further minute. Transfer to a serving dish and keep warm.

Serve the bread and butter pudding with chocolate sauce drizzled over the top. Serving with whipped cream is strongly advised.

MANGO YOGHURT CAKE

SERVES 6–8

230 g (8 oz) unsalted butter

240 g (8½ oz/1 cup) caster (superfine) sugar

2 teaspoons vanilla paste

3 whole eggs

190 g (6½ oz/1⅔ cups) self-raising flour, sifted

60 g (2 oz/½ cup) almond meal, sifted

250 g (9 oz/1 cup) Greek-style yoghurt

2 tablespoons milk

400 g (14 oz) fresh mango pieces, drained mangos in syrup will also work

icing (confectioner's) sugar, for dusting, to serve

whipped cream or crème fraîche, to serve

Preheat oven to 170 °C (340 °F) and grease and line the bottom of a 23 cm spring-form cake tin.

Using an electric mixer cream the butter, sugar and vanilla paste until pale and fluffy, around 5–7 minutes. With the electric mixer running, add one egg at a time and combine. Do not add the next egg until the one before is completely incorporated into the butter.

Once the eggs are mixed, use a spatula to gently fold in the flour, almond meal, milk and yoghurt until just combined. Gently fold the mango pieces through and pour the batter into the prepared cake tin.

Bake for 1–1⅓ hours, or until a skewer comes out clean when inserted into the centre. If the cake starts to brown too quickly, cover it with aluminium foil to finish the cooking.

When cooked, cool the cake completely on a cake rack before removing from the cake tin. Dust with icing (confectioner's) sugar and serve with cream or crème fraîche.

PUFTALOONS WITH WILD HONEY

SERVES 4–6

This is a very old recipe. As a kid we called them 'puftaloonies' and my dad would use them as a skills test for any potential camp cooks. If the applying camp cook couldn't produce these then he/she really limited their chances of getting a job in our stock camp. Not only would we use lard as the wet ingredient when making the dough, we would also cook these in straight lard. Obviously, I don't want to give you a heart attack, so I use melted butter in the batter and a neutral oil for frying, such as vegetable oil.

1 litre (34 fl oz/4 cups) vegetable oil, for frying
200 g (7 oz/1⅓ cups) self-raising flour
40 g (1½ oz/¼ cup) milk powder
1 tablespoon caster (superfine) sugar
50 g (1¾ oz) unsalted butter, melted
130 ml (4½ fl oz/½ cup) full-cream (whole) milk, at room temperature

Heat the oil in a medium-sized pot to 180 °C (350 °F). If you don't have a thermometer, the oil is at frying temperature when a piece of bread turns golden brown in 20 seconds when dropped in.

Sift the dry ingredients into a medium-sized mixing bowl. Make a well in the centre and add the wet ingredients. Gently fold together until a soft, sticky dough has formed.

Fry tablespoon-sized chunks of dough in the hot oil, being careful when you place them into the oil to avoid splashing the hot oil about. Flip the puftaloons while they are cooking to ensure even cooking. Remove the puftaloons with a slotted spoon after 3–4 minutes. They should be golden brown and cooked through.

Drain them on paper towel and serve while still hot, with your choice of jam, honey or golden syrup. (I use wild honey from Humpty Doo, in particular, a honey that is collected in the wet season. It is a deep brown colour which has hints of golden syrup in it.)

GOLDEN SYRUP DUMPLINGS WITH A DASH OF TOFFEE

I grew up eating these and I absolutely love them. I make a bitter toffee in this recipe then stir in the hot golden syrup. It is a little grown-up and helps cut through the rich syrup. I also bake my dumplings because I like a little golden crunch on the top, however boiling them on the stove will work just fine.

DUMPLINGS

150 g (5½ oz/1 cup) self-raising flour
75 g (2¾ oz/½ cup) plain (all-purpose) flour
50 g (1¾ oz) unsalted butter, at room temperature
2 tablespoons caster (superfine) sugar
190 ml (6½ fl oz/¾ cup) milk

SAUCE

100 g (3½ oz/½ cup) brown sugar
250 ml (8½ fl oz/1 cup) water
80 ml (2½ fl oz/⅓ cup) golden syrup
115 g (4 oz/½ cup) caster (superfine) sugar
60 g (2 oz) unsalted butter

Preheat oven to 180 °C (350 °F).

In a food processor blend the flour, butter and sugar on high until the mix resembles bread crumbs. Transfer to a mixing bowl and make a well in the centre. Pour the milk into the well and combine with a spatula until a soft dough has formed. Don't overwork the dough—as soon as the dough has formed stop mixing.

Divide the dumpling dough into tablespoon-sized balls and place on a tray lined with baking paper.

In a small saucepan, over medium heat, combine the brown sugar, water and golden syrup, and bring to boil. Keep it hot. In a large ovenproof dish with a lid add the sugar with a small amount of water until it resembles wet sand. Cook the sugar over high heat until it starts to caramelise, 8–10 minutes—you want to make a bitter toffee, so when the toffee turns from golden to brown it is ready.

Take the toffee off the heat and, being very careful, whisk the butter into the toffee. The butter will make the toffee bubble up so be very careful not to burn yourself. Return the pot to the heat and, while whisking, slowly pour in the golden syrup mix.

Place the dumplings into the pot and put the lid on. Bake in the oven for 25 minutes, or until a skewer comes out clean when inserted into the centre of a dumpling. Remove the lid for the last 10 minutes of cooking time.

BOB'S OUTBACK STEAMED PUDDING WITH COCONUT CARAMEL

85 g (3 oz/½ cup) self-raising flour

60 g (2 oz/½ cup) almond meal

120 g (4½ oz) unsalted butter, at room temperature

115 g (3½ oz/½ cup) caster (superfine) sugar

2 eggs, at room temperature

1 teaspoon baking powder

2 tablespoons quandong, finely chopped

1 tablespoon native currants, normal currants can be used

1 tablespoon dried apricots, finely chopped

2 teaspoons wattle seed

2 tablespoons full-cream (whole) milk

CARAMEL

150 g (5½ oz/1 cup) caster (superfine) sugar

45 g (1½ oz) unsalted butter

90 ml (3 fl oz/⅓ cup) coconut cream

Preheat oven to 180 °C (350 °F) and grease 6 × 150 ml (5 fl oz) moulds.

Sift the flour, almond meal and baking powder into a mixing bowl.

In another bowl use an electric mixer to cream the butter and sugar until pale and fluffy, around 5–7 minutes. Beat in the eggs one at a time. Do not add the next egg until the previous one is completely incorporated. Using a spatula, gently fold in the dry ingredients, fruit and wattle seed, adding milk as you go.

Spoon the mixture into the greased moulds, then stand them in an ovenproof dish lined with a tea towel. Pour boiling water into the dish until it comes two-thirds up the moulds. Cover the dish tightly with aluminium foil and bake for 30–35 minutes, or until a skewer comes out clean when inserted into the centre of the puddings. Allow the puddings to cool slightly before removing them from the moulds and serving.

Meanwhile, make the caramel. This caramel uses the same technique as a normal caramel with just the substitution of coconut cream instead of cows cream. Place the sugar into a frying pan over high heat with just enough water added to make it look like wet sand. Cook the sugar without stirring until it starts to caramelise, 8–10 minutes. As the sugar starts to caramelise you may have to agitate the pan to ensure even cooking. When the sugar is a deep golden brown colour take it off the heat and very carefully whisk in the butter and coconut cream. Transfer to a serving bowl and keep warm.

Serve the steamed puddings topped with coconut caramel.

NATIVE INGREDIENTS
Bob (Penunka) Taylor

All around the world people are putting an emphasis back on their heritage and native ingredients, and why not? The Australian continent is home to a wide array of edible fruits, tubers, leaves, fungi and animals that number into the thousands.

A man who is an expert in native Australian food is my good friend Bob, or Penunka, a trained chef of twenty-six years who has worked all over Australia, as well as in Europe. Bob now lives and works in the Red Centre, guiding people through the native Australian bush, using his skill as a trained chef to cook incredible food over a fire while talking about the Aboriginal history of Australia and the adaptation of their culture in modern times.

Bob's family are traditional owners of the Rainbow Valley in Central Australia and have gathered and eaten native Australian

ingredients for thousands of years. Bob uses a lot of native ingredients in his cooking, which to Bob is an obvious choice considering his heritage. Possibly his signature dish, and one of my favourites, is his native steamed pudding with coconut caramel. He wouldn't part with his secret recipe, however I have given it a go.

VANILLA ICE-CREAM WITH POACHED ROSELLA

Unless you know someone who has some, or you pick it yourself, fresh rosella is a tricky ingredient to source. If you can't get your hands on fresh rosella you can buy it already prepared from specialty food stores as 'wild hibiscus in syrup'.

200 ml (7 fl oz/¾ cup) full-cream (whole) milk
300 ml (10 fl oz/1¼ cups) full (whole) cream
2 tablespoons glucose
2 vanilla pods, split and seeds scraped
¼ teaspoon freshly ground coffee
5 egg yolks
80 g (2¾ oz/⅓ cup) caster (superfine) sugar

ROSELLA

100 g (3½ oz) fresh rosella, thoroughly washed and seeds removed (2 per serve)
100 g (3½ oz/½ cup) caster (superfine) sugar
100 ml (3½ fl oz/⅓ cup) water
pinch of saffron threads

Prepare your ice-cream churner according to the manufacturer's instructions.

To make the vanilla ice-cream heat the milk, cream, glucose, vanilla pods and seeds, along with the coffee in a pot, over a low–medium heat, stirring occasionally until just before it reaches boiling point. Set aside and let steep for 20–25 minutes.

In a medium mixing bowl whisk the egg yolks until pale and fluffy. Add the sugar and whisk for a further 2–3 minutes. Slowly pour the cream and vanilla mixture into the yolks. Whisk to incorporate.

Prepare an ice bath.

Transfer the ice-cream base to a medium heavy-based pot. Using a thermometer, and stirring continually, bring the temperature to 82 °C (180 °F). Strain the ice-cream base immediately into a bowl sitting in the ice bath and discard the solids. When the ice-cream base is cool, churn according to the manufacturer's instructions.

While the ice-cream is churning, prepare the rosella syrup. In a small saucepan combine all the ingredients for the syrup and simmer gently for 10–15 minutes, or until the rosella just starts to soften.

Serve the vanilla ice-cream with rosella flowers and a generous helping of the syrup.

THE EASIEST MANGO ICE-CREAM

SERVES 6

Towards the end of mango season the entire Top End starts to freeze all their mangoes. If you have a tree I highly recommend spending some time freezing some mangoes as you will have great quality frozen mango all year round ... If you don't have a mango tree, make friends with someone that does or buy up big when they are at the end of the season and cheap.

500 g (1 lb 2 oz) frozen mango
squeeze of lemon juice
80 ml (2½ fl oz/⅓ cup) full
  (whole) cream

In a food processor blitz the frozen mango, lemon juice and cream on high for 1–2 minutes, or until completely smooth. You want to process it for as little time as possible because the longer it's blitzed, the softer it becomes.

Serve immediately. I buy good quality waffle cones and serve a scoop of mango ice-cream in each cone.

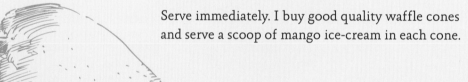

BUFFALO MILK ICE-CREAM

1 LITRE

Buffalo milk has an incredible flavour. For this recipe I wanted to keep things simple so that the rich, creamy and delicate taste isn't lost under a pile of other ingredients and flavours. This ice-cream is beautiful simply on its own, however it works just as well with poached fruit of any description — one of my favourites is poached peaches with cinnamon and brown sugar. While having an ice-cream churner makes the process very easy, it is not essential — you will just need to have some spare time and be willing to put in a bit of hard work and you can achieve a near perfect result. See below recipe for tips on how to make this ice-cream without an ice-cream machine.

750 ml (25½ fl oz /3 cups) buffalo milk
2 tablespoons glucose
100 g (3½ oz/½ cup) caster (superfine) sugar
70 g (2½ oz) full-cream (whole) powdered milk

Following the manufacturer's instructions, prepare your ice-cream churner.

In a large saucepan combine all your ingredients and heat them gently over low heat, stirring continually. Once the ingredients have dissolved, take the saucepan off the heat and cool the mixture over an ice bath, then transfer it to your ice-cream machine and churn according to the manufacturer's instructions.

If you don't have an ice-cream machine you will need the following: a deep baking tray or large durable bowl, a whisk and freezer space. After the recipe base has been made transfer the mixture to the tray or bowl and pop it into the freezer. After about 45 minutes remove the bowl from the freezer to check the mixture, as it starts to freeze from this point. Whisk the ice-cream vigorously for about 30 seconds to break up the ice crystals. Pop the mix back into the freezer and repeat the whisking process every 30 minutes until the ice-cream is frozen. The more effort that is applied at this stage the smoother and creamier the end result will be. The entire process should take between 2½ and 3 hours to complete.

SEMIFREDDO WITH STRAWBERRY RIPPLE

SERVES 6–8

Semifreddo is best eaten on the day you make it. Prepare this on the morning of the day you plan to serve it. It needs at least 5–6 hours of freezing time.

6 egg whites
230 g (8 oz/1 cup) caster (superfine) sugar
½ teaspoon cream of tartar
500 ml (17 fl oz/2 cups) full (whole) cream, cold and whipped to soft peaks
1½ teaspoons freshly ground black pepper

RIPPLE

300 g (10½ oz) strawberries, hulled
80 g (2¾ oz/⅓ cup) caster (superfine) sugar
2 tablespoons glucose
3 teaspoons balsamic vinegar

In a food processor blend all the ingredients for the strawberry ripple on high for 2–3 minutes, or until a smooth consistency is reached. Pass the liquid through a sieve into a small pot and gently heat until all the sugar has dissolved. Cool in the fridge until you are ready to put the ripple through the semifreddo base.

In a saucepan, over medium heat, bring the sugar to boil with a cup of water, stirring with a wooden spoon until the sugar dissolves and reaches 115 °C (239 °F), 10–15 minutes. Brush any sugar crystals from the side with a clean, wet pastry bush and keep sugar at 115 °C (239 °F).

Use a food processor on low to whip the egg whites until they are frothy. Add the cream of tartar and continue to whip the egg whites until soft peaks have formed.

Now increase the heat of the sugar to high and bring the temperature up to 121 °C (250 °F). At the same time increase the speed of the motor to high and with motor running gradually pour in the hot sugar syrup. Reduce the motor speed to medium and beat until the meringue is stiff and glossy and at room temperature.

Line a 2 litre (68 fl oz) capacity tin with plastic wrap.

In a large mixing bowl gently fold the Italian meringue and black pepper into the whipped cream, a third at a time, until fully incorporated.

Drizzle half of the strawberry ripple over the semifreddo and fold in until rippled through the entire semifreddo. Pour into prepared tin and freeze for at least 5–6 hours.

To serve, garnish with the remaining strawberry syrup.

INDEX

ABOUT THE AUTHOR

Having grown up on a cattle farm in the Northern Territory, Lynton Tapp's first big break came when he became a contestant on the successful *MasterChef* TV show in series 5. Touted as the 'Stockman', Lynton quickly became a firm favourite and built a social media following of over 20,000. Since the show, Lynton has become Foodbank Victoria's first ambassador and delivered food to bushfire-affected areas of Victoria. He's also spent time cooking in the kitchen of fine-dining restaurant Pei Modern in Melbourne, and acts as an ambassador for Tourism NT. Most recently, Lynton has been involved in Tourism Australia's new initiative Restaurant Australia, which brought him to London to cook for the Duchess of Cornwall on Australia Day in 2015. Lynton is a proud country boy who seeks to champion the efforts of Australia's tireless food producers.

AUTHOR'S ACKNOWLEDGEMENTS

There is an enormous amount of work that goes into publishing a book, and this book is no different. I would like to say thank you to all of the people involved in the making of this beautiful book.

To my family: Mum, Dad, Eric, Courtney and Emily. As you would expect, my family have been my biggest supporters. I honestly believe that without their continued encouragement I wouldn't have been able to see through the tough times in Melbourne and do all that I have done.

Steve, Jill, Nick and Louise Spargo. The Spargos have helped me find my feet in Melbourne. They have continually supported me and I will be forever grateful for the kindness and generosity they have shown me.

Matt Germanchis, an incredible mentor and now a great friend. I have been extremely fortunate to learn from Matt, undoubtedly one of the best chefs in Australia. Thank you for everything Matt.

Glenn, Iana, Ian, Jayde and Nigel, my second family. Without these amazing people I wouldn't have got to where I am. My closest and dearest friends in the world—when you have people like this in your life it makes you realise how lucky you are.

My amazing publisher Explore Australia. Without all the help and guidance from the amazing team—Alison, Melissa, Martine, Katy, Julie and Tash—*Outback Pantry* wouldn't quite be the beautiful book that it is.

I want to thank Tourism NT and, in particular, Kate and Richard who have been amazing in their support of me. Another special thank you to Shaana who took all the incredible photos of the Northern Territory producers.

Lastly, this book would not have come together without all of the farmers and producers I have written about. A very big thank you to: Jimmy Shu, Craig Zwetsloot, John Shaw, Carmel and Ziko, Billy and Pam Bousted, the Richards at Humpty Doo Barramundi, Stu Beckett, Chris Yates, Daniel and Shannon Tapp, Patrick Carmody, Sharon and Geoff Arthurs, Traci McHours and Bob Taylor.

ACKNOWLEDGEMENTS

The publisher would like to acknowledge the following individuals and organisations:

Editorial manager
Melissa Kayser

Project manager
Alison Proietto

Editor
Martine Lleonart

Food economist
Grace Campbell

Food stylist
Katy Holder

Cover design
Penny Black Design & Mark Campbell

Design and layout
Penny Black Design

Pre-press
Splitting Image

Photography credits
Front cover: Tourism NT
Title page: Tourism NT
Back cover: Tourism NT

All other images © Natasha Milne

Except for pages: vi–vii, x–xi, xii–1, 12, 13, 18, 26–7, 28–29, 38, 39, 42, 43, 48, 49, 56–7, 58–9, 66, 67, 72, 73, 78, 79, 84–5, 86–7, 94, 95, 102–3, 112–3, 116–7, 124, 125, 132, 133, 136–7, 142–3, 152, 153, 156–7, 162, 163, 170–1, 174, 178–179, 180 Tourism NT

Illustrations and some backgrounds appearing throughout this book were sourced from the following artists on Shutterstock.com: Alena Kaz; andrey oleyniik; bioraven; Boonsom; Canicula; Cbenjasuwan; geraria; grafnata; happydancing; itVega; Knopazyzy; KUCO; La puma; lenaalyonushka; Liliya Shlapak; Loco; Macrovector; Marina99; Matee Nuserm; melazerg; Mr.prasong; Muskoka Stock Photos; nednapa; Nikiparonak; Nikiteev_Konstantin; Roobcio; somchai rakin; Yatra;

Explore Australia Publishing Pty Ltd
Ground Floor, Building 1, 658 Church Street, Richmond, VIC 3121

Explore Australia Publishing Pty Ltd is a division of Hardie Grant Publishing Pty Ltd

hardie grant publishing

Published by Explore Australia Publishing Pty Ltd, 2015

Form and design © Explore Australia Publishing Pty Ltd, 2015
Concept and text © Lynton Tapp, 2015

A Cataloguing-in-Publication entry is available from the catalogue of the National Library of Australia at www.nla.gov.au

ISBN-13 9781741174885

10 9 8 7 6 5 4 3 2 1

Printed and bound in China by 1010 Printing International Ltd

Disclaimer: This book uses metric cup measurements, i.e. 250 ml for 1 cup; in the US 1 cup is 8 fl oz, just smaller, and American cooks should be generous in their cup measurements; in the UK 1 cup is 10 fl oz, and British cooks should be scant with their cup measurements.

Publisher's note: Every effort has been made to ensure that the information in this book is accurate at the time of going to press. The publisher welcomes information and suggestions for correction or improvement. Email: info@exploreaustralia.net.au

www.exploreaustralia.net.au
Follow us on Twitter: @ExploreAus
Find us on Facebook: www.facebook.com/exploreaustralia